REFORMING ENVIRONMENTAL REGULATION IN OECD COUNTRIES

ORGANISATION FOR ECONOMIC CO-OPERATION AND DEVELOPMENT

ORGANISATION FOR ECONOMIC CO-OPERATION AND DEVELOPMENT

Pursuant to Article 1 of the Convention signed in Paris on 14th December 1960, and which came into force on 30th September 1961, the Organisation for Economic Co-operation and Development (OECD) shall promote policies designed:

- to achieve the highest sustainable economic growth and employment and a rising standard of living in Member countries, while maintaining financial stability, and thus to contribute to the development of the world economy;
- to contribute to sound economic expansion in Member as well as non-member countries in the process of economic development; and
- to contribute to the expansion of world trade on a multilateral, non-discriminatory basis in accordance with international obligations.

The original Member countries of the OECD are Austria, Belgium, Canada, Denmark, France, Germany, Greece, Iceland, Ireland, Italy, Luxembourg, the Netherlands, Norway, Portugal, Spain, Sweden, Switzerland, Turkey, the United Kingdom and the United States. The following countries became Members subsequently through accession at the dates indicated hereafter: Japan (28th April 1964), Finland (28th January 1969), Australia (7th June 1971), New Zealand (29th May 1973), Mexico (18th May 1994), the Czech Republic (21st December 1995), Hungary (7th May 1996), Poland (22nd November 1996) and the Republic of Korea (12th December 1996). The Commission of the European Communities takes part in the work of the OECD (Article 13 of the OECD Convention).

Publié en français sous le titre :

RÉFORMER LA RÉGLEMENTATION ENVIRONNEMENTALE DANS LES PAYS DE L'OCDE

FOREWORD

Following a request of the 1995 OECD Council meeting at Ministerial level, requesting OECD to "examine the significance, direction, and means of reform in regulatory regimes", the OECD carried out a horizontal study on regulatory reform in various sectors of activity. This report has been prepared by Prof. Norman LEE (University of Manchester) in this context, and reviewed by both the Group on Economic and Environment Policy Integration and the Environment Policy Committee. It is published on the responsibility of the Secretary-General of the OECD.

TABLE OF CONTENTS

List of Boxes

INTRODUCTION

The purpose of this report is to review the objectives, strategies and achievements of regulatory reform, relating to environmental policy, in OECD countries and to suggest ways in which the process of regulatory reform in this policy area may be strengthened in the future.

The report has been prepared, between November 1996 and February 1997, in parallel with the later stages of the Regulatory Reform Review requested by the Council of the OECD in March 1995 (OECD, 1995a). Whilst it has not constituted part of that Review, which is broader in scope but has not primarily addressed environmental and social regulatory reform issues, it has considered similar basic questions and adopted broadly comparable evaluative criteria (OECD, 1996a). In the process, it has made use of a number of the background reports which have been produced as a basis for the substantive report on Regulatory Reform for the 1997 Meeting of the Council at Ministerial Level, in addition to very considerable documentation from the Environment Directorate and other sources on environmental regulation and its reform.

The report is divided into four main sections:

1. *Scope and Rationale of Environmental Regulatory Reform.* This includes: the scope and types of environmental regulations which are covered in the report; the case for environmental regulation and its reform; and the linkages between environmental regulatory reform (ERR) and general regulatory reform (RR).

2. *Progress in Environmental Regulatory Reform.* This reviews recent, ongoing and prospective measures of ERR in OECD countries, distinguishing between: command and control instruments; economic instruments; and other (voluntary, planning etc.) instruments. The overall impacts of ERR, and linkages between ERR and RR in overall appraisal, are also examined.

3. *Role of Regulatory Impact Analysis in Environmental Regulatory Reform.* This reviews the progress made in OECD countries in appraising new environmental

regulations and evaluating existing environmental regulations as part of the environmental regulatory reform process.

4. *Conclusions and Recommendations.* The chapter summarises the principal conclusions of the review of ERR in OECD countries and presents a number of suggestions for strengthening the ERR process in the future.

Section 1

SCOPE AND RATIONALE OF ENVIRONMENTAL REGULATORY REFORM

1.1 The scope of environmental regulatory systems

The term "regulation" is defined differently (either more narrowly or more broadly) in different contexts. For the purpose of this report it has been broadly defined as in the Regulatory Reform Review (see Box 1), but encompassing the regulation of public sector, as well as private sector, behaviour.

Box 1. Definitions of "regulation" in the OECD regulatory reform study

"Although there is no accepted international definition of regulation, the term 'regulation' is used broadly in this document to include the full range of legal instruments by which governing institutions, at all levels of government, impose obligations or constraints on private sector behaviour. Constitutions, parliamentary laws, subordinate legislation, decrees, orders, norms, licenses, plans, codes and even some forms of administrative guidance can all be considered as regulation." ["Recommendation of the Council of the OECD on Improving the Quality of Government Regulation", (1995*a*), p. 20].

"Regulations can include both formal legal instruments and more informal instruments, such as guidance, that are issued by all levels of government. 'Regulation' in this work can also include rules issued by non-governmental bodies, such as self-regulatory bodies, to whom governments have delegated regulatory powers." [*Regulatory Reform: Overview and Proposed* OECD *Work Plan*, (1996*a*), p. 4].

The main types of environmental regulation which fall within the scope of this definition have been grouped into three categories; these, together with examples of their principal components, are shown in Box 2. These illustrate the considerable range and diversity of policy instruments in use in OECD countries. The listings are not exhaustive nor is this a rigid classification. For example, some instruments may be "hybrids" containing features drawn from more than one category (*e.g.* command and control/voluntary; economic/voluntary).

1.2 The case for environmental regulation and its reform

The justification for environmental regulation lies in market failures causing environmental externalities which are only automatically internalised in

---

Box 2. **Categories and sub-categories of environmental regulatory instruments in OECD countries**

1. **Command and control instruments**

   These directly regulate behaviour affecting the environment, typically through permit and authorisation procedures relating to the following:

   a) the products produced and distributed;

   b) the materials used in production and distribution;

   c) the technologies by which goods and materials are produced;

   d) the residuals which are released into the environment;

   e) the locations at which production and other economic activities take place.

2. **Economic instruments**

   These modify behaviour, using financial incentives and disincentives, to improve environmental performance through:

   a) charges and taxes;

   b) grants and subsidies;

   c) fines etc. for non-compliance;

   d) market creation mechanisms, such as emission permit trading schemes.

3. **Other instruments**

   These, often containing a non-mandatory element, aim to improve environmental performance by *i*) improving the supply of information relating to environmental problems and the ways of reducing them, and *ii*) raising the level of voluntary commitment, both at an individual organisation and collective level, to modify practices to reduce these problems. Elements of this approach are to be found in the following examples (although they also often contain elements of the other approaches):

   a) environmental planning, environmental impact assessment, life cycle assessment and related extended producer responsibility procedures;

   b) voluntary individual and association agreements to promote environmental policy objectives through industry covenants, negotiated agreements, self-regulation, codes of conduct and eco-audits;

   c) information disclosure schemes (voluntary or compulsory);

   d) environmental management systems and environmental audit procedures to improve cost-effective compliance with agreed environmental quality targets.

decision-making in perfectly competitive markets. Unfortunately, these idealised market systems are not fully realisable in practice. Nor, as demonstrated in the theory of the second best, does a movement towards greater competition, which falls short of perfect competition, necessarily reduce environmental problems, let alone resolve them (Lipsey and Lancaster, 1956).

Therefore, the objective of environmental regulation is to change market behaviour in ways which are more closely consistent with behaviour when externalities are internalised, using methods which are feasible and cost-effective and which have acceptable distributional effects. However, this objective is often imperfectly achieved – in other words, *regulatory failure* occurs. This, in turn, provides the need and justification for environmental regulatory reform.

The objectives of environmental regulatory reform and general regulatory reform are compatible with each other if each is carefully defined. However, the *means* by which each is achieved, and the degree of reliance to be placed on different reform measures, may differ. This is reflected in the following extract from the OECD paper "Regulatory Reform: Overview and Proposed Work Plan" in Box 3 below.

Box 3. **Key considerations in regulatory reform**

"The key questions underlying reform are neutral and do not preclude a pro-active regulatory role for government. They are: Are regulatory costs justified by benefits? Does regulatory intervention produce more social and economic benefits than would alternatives? Are regulations designed to achieve policy objectives at lowest costs? These questions are reflected in two major thrusts of regulatory reform in OECD countries: i) increasing market incentives for efficiency and innovations, and ii) improving regulatory quality where protective regulations are needed.

i)   *Where competition can produce greater benefits* (our emphasis), reform requires, as a first priority, the targeted dismantling of barriers to entry and exit, of price controls, and of other restrictions on competition...

ii) Many regulations produce important social benefits by remedying market failures in such areas as environmental and consumer protection... [However], in many cases, social objectives can be achieved at lower cost by changing regulatory approaches, that is by using more efficient means to intervene in markets" [OECD (1996a), *Regulatory Reform: Overview and Proposed Work Plan*, p. 4-6].

Hence, environmental regulatory reform should be driven by a combined consideration of the *environmental benefits* it may yield and the *regulatory cost savings/dissavings* and *distributional effects* which may result. The choice of reform instruments, market liberalising and/or regulation modifying, should be subordinate to this.

1.3 Linkages between environmental regulatory reform and general regulatory reform

It is also important that interdependencies between the environmental regulatory system and other regulatory systems are sufficiently recognised in the reform process.

The key linkages are shown in Figure 1 which also illustrates how incomplete coverage may result in biased evaluations, for example:

a) an economically-oriented reform process may over-focus on B and C consequences;

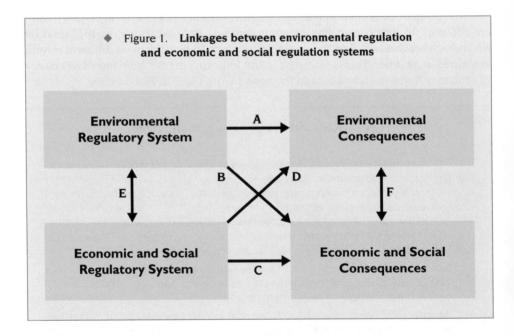

◆ Figure 1. **Linkages between environmental regulation and economic and social regulation systems**

b) an environmentally-oriented reform process may over-focus on A and D consequences; and

c) both reform processes may neglect E and F consequences (*e.g.* the influence of changes in economic and social regulations on the effectiveness of environmental regulations [E consequences] and the influence of environmental changes on economic and social impacts [F consequences].

Taking inter-sectoral linkages into consideration is fully consistent with OECD policy "to pursue the integration of environmental with economic and other policies" (OECD, 1996*b*, Communiqué, p. 3). However, to achieve this satisfactorily is a considerable challenge for the regulatory process as a whole.

Section 2

PROGRESS IN ENVIRONMENTAL REGULATORY REFORM

2.1 Introductory overview

According to the Environment Directorate's Survey on Environmental Regulatory Reform, ERR processes are underway in virtually all of the responding Member countries* (Environment Directorate, 1996). In some cases reforms are primarily being undertaken to improve environmental effectiveness and are being initiated by the Member country's environment ministry. In certain other cases they are part of a more general regulatory review process and may be driven by other government departments. In these cases, the primary objective may be to improve overall economic performance, with such sub-objectives as increasing competitiveness, stimulating technical progress and innovation, promoting international trade, increasing the economic growth rate and reducing unemployment. In a third group of cases, the reform process is expected to serve a mixture of environmental, social and economic objectives, although the relationships between these, and the constituent regulatory instruments which they use, may not always be well-defined.

Environmental regulatory reform is not new. From at least the late 1960s, there has been, in most Member countries, an almost continuous process of environmental regulatory change in response to changing environmental pressures associated with such factors as economic growth, structural adjustment, changing technology, globalisation, institutional change and increased environmental awareness (see Box A.1 for further details). Much of this has been driven by a perceived need for greater environmental effectiveness but, particularly during periods of economic difficulty and especially during the 1990s, it has also been associated with concerns over the costs of environmental regulation and the economic consequences which may flow from these.

---

* The Member countries responding to the Environment Directorate's survey were: Austria, Belgium, Canada, Czech Republic, Denmark, Hungary, Iceland, Japan, Mexico, Netherlands, Norway, Portugal, Spain, Sweden, Turkey, United Kingdom, United States and the European Commission.

Throughout the period, environmental regulatory systems in Member countries have been predominantly based on the use of command and control regulatory instruments. For this reason, it is often assumed that, there has been little fundamental innovation in the regulatory systems over the past thirty years. However, without minimising any deficiencies in existing systems, it is worth noting that there have been a number of important improvements, of both environmental and economic significance, *within* command and control systems over this period. Also, there has been increased use of economic and other instruments, *in conjunction with* command and control instruments, in "hybrid" or "packaged" environmental regulatory systems.

The main types of traditional and new instruments are reviewed below, by broad category, and then their combined effects are evaluated, to the extent that existing information permits.

2.2 Command and control instruments

At the core of the command and control system, in all Member countries, is a set of direct regulations relating to polluting and resource use activities. An OECD

Box 4.   Deficiencies in command and control systems, 1970-85

- Multiplication of regulations had occurred which, in some instances, had become burdensome and was increasing difficulties in achieving adequate and efficient enforcement.

- There was a tendency for regulations to be poorly co-ordinated – for example, addressing specific pollution problems in a single environmental medium without adequately considering inter-relationships between environmental media.

- A too narrow focus on conventional, point source pollutants and local/regional environmental quality problems.

- Emphasis on "react and cure" policies in contrast to "anticipate and prevent" strategies.

- Little consideration was given to the inter-dependence between environmental policy and policies in other economic sectors.

- Other types of policy instruments, such as financial incentives and disincentives, although they existed were only used in a relatively small number of cases.

Source: OECD (1987), *Improving the Enforcement of Environmental Policies*, Environment Monograph No. 8.

study in the late 1980s reviewed the development of that system, primarily from the perspective of its enforcement, over the period 1970-85 (OECD, 1987). Although considerable progress had been recorded in containing or reducing individual pollution problems through this system, it was acknowledged that it still displayed a number of deficiencies (see Box 4).

In response to this situation, the authors of the monograph recommended overall improvements to the entire environmental management cycle in the following ways:

- feed-back mechanisms should be introduced and strengthened to stimulate adjustments and ongoing improvements to the systems in use;
- there should be fewer and simpler regulations;
- there should be simpler and faster procedures for using permits;
- monitoring systems and monitoring procedures should be improved including the development of self-monitoring and the use of indirect measurements for small discharges;
- co-operative agreements with industry should be promoted and publicised;
- the use of environmental auditing procedures should be encouraged;
- there should be more effective sanctions, with fines at a sufficient level to act as a deterrent;
- command and control regulations should be supported by the use of additional instruments such as economic instruments and other incentives;
- fuller information and wider publicity should be provided to polluters on pollution control techniques and policies, and more information should be supplied to the public on discharges, sanctions and success stories;
- the capabilities of the enforcement agencies should be strengthened through the more rational allocation of tasks, better staff training etc. [Source: OECD (1987) *op. cit.*].

In many respects, these suggestions reflected the prevailing thinking in Member countries on the main ways in which command and control systems should be (and in certain cases, already were being) reformed, and should be supplemented by the use of economic and other instruments, on both environmental and cost-effectiveness grounds.

This type of approach was broadly endorsed by OECD Ministers in their 1991 Communiqué, when setting the goal of reducing the OECD area's overall pollution burden during the 1990s. In this statement, they acknowledged that more comprehensive and integrative policy approaches, based upon the preventive principle, would be needed to sustain overall environmental improvements in economies which were expected to continue expanding (OECD, 1991).

17

This led, in the OECD Report (1994a), *Reducing Environmental Pollution: Looking Back, Thinking Ahead*, to the conclusion that governments should clarify:

a) where and how traditional command and control instruments worked best, and

b) which newer anticipatory and integrative policy instruments should be developed in a complementary role.

Among the latter were identified, as possible candidates, economic instruments, environmental planning and evaluation, integrated pollution prevention and control, integrated life cycle assessment and integrated resource planning (OECD, 1994a).

During the 1990s, the ERR process, in a number of OECD countries, has been addressing many of the above issues, leading to improvements *within* and *beyond* the command and control systems currently in place. The types of improvements which have been made are indicated below and certain of these are illustrated more fully in the boxes located in the Annex to this report.

● The need to retain existing regulations has been reviewed leading to the termination, consolidation or simplification of certain regulations (see Box A.2, Environment Canada: Regulatory Review, 1992-94 and Box A.3, Environmental Regulatory Reform in the European Union).

● Conscious efforts have been made to simplify bureaucratic procedures and paper work associated with particular regulations (see Box 5, Regulatory Reform Programme of USEPA).

● Greater flexibility has been introduced in the choice of means by which standards are to be achieved in order to reduce technological rigidities and to promote more cost-effective compliance (see Box A.4, Some Characteristics of Industrial Permitting Systems in OECD Countries).

● Integrated permitting procedures are being introduced with a consequential simplification of procedures accompanied, in some cases, by institutional consolidation (see Box A.5, Integrated Pollution Prevention and Control in OECD Countries).

● Strengthening of environmental planning by developers has been encouraged through the integration of mandatory environmental impact assessment (EIA) procedures within command and control permitting systems (see review of EIA developments in Section 2.4, "Other Instruments" below).

Box 5. **Environmental regulatory reform in the United States:**
some examples

President Clinton issued a report *Reinventing Environmental Regulation* in March 1995. EPA's response, summarised in the slogan "cleaner, cheaper, smarter", encompasses a number of initiatives such as:

● *Reducing paperwork and cutting red tape.* 1 400 pages of obsolete environmental rules are to be eliminated. 10 million hours of paperwork and red tape for large and small businesses seeking to comply with environmental laws have been eliminated; a further 10 million hours of paperwork were due to be eliminated by the end of 1996.

● *Making it easier for businesses to comply with environmental laws* through common sense compliance incentives, for small businesses on the Environmental Leadership Programme, to enhance businesses' ability to meet environmental requirements through innovative approaches; funding of Small Business Compliance Centres for the metal finishing, printing, automotive repair and farming industries.

● *Using innovation and flexibility to achieve better environmental results.* Providing flexibility and cutting red tape to find the cheapest and most efficient ways to achieve higher environmental performance standards.

● Basing environmental regulations on *environmental performance goals*, whilst providing maximum flexibility in the means of achieving these.

● *Increasing community participation and partnerships* through expanding public access to Agency information, establishing Performance Partnerships to combine federal funds to meet environmental needs and partnerships between EPA, industry and other groups to improve drinking water safety.

● Enact *simpler regulations*, understandable to those affected.

● Promote *"environmental justice"*, *i.e.* an equitable distribution of costs and benefits.

● Encourage *self-policing* by companies and voluntary systems.

● Implement "place-based programmes", *i.e.* taking an ecosystem as the basis for designing a management strategy (rather than an approach based on administrative boundaries).

Source: *Re-inventing Environmental Regulation*, 1996, US Environmental Protection Agency, Environment Directorate Survey and OECD (1996q)

● Minimum and maximum time limits have been set for certain procedural stages (*e.g.* consultation and public participation) in some command and control systems.

● Greater opportunities have been provided for developer-authority consultation within the framework of command and control systems (*e.g.* when reviewing the operation of existing regulations, developing revised and new regulations and identifying the most cost-effective ways of achieving environmental quality objectives).

● Increasing non-compliance fines and raising permit application charges to cover permitting costs etc. to strengthen compliance incentives and to provide additional finance for the more effective operation of permitting systems.

In the Netherlands, the continuing evolution of the environmental regulatory system from a traditional command and control system to a hybrid system and, eventually, to a predominantly voluntary agreement system, is envisaged by some to be a long-term regulatory reform goal. This is illustrated in Box 6 which distinguishes four possible phases in the development of the Dutch environmental regulatory system. According to the authors, most Dutch companies are currently judged to be in, or around, Phase 2. It is noteworthy that a regulatory system is still expected to be in place in Phase 4, although its form and function should have changed considerably from one based on coercion to one largely reliant on mutual trust.

How far this long-term goal might be realised within the OECD area as a whole, and over what time frame, could be a topic of lively discussion and debate within the Member countries.

2.3 Economic instruments

Introduction

Economic instruments of environmental policy comprise those policy instruments which may influence environmental outcomes by changing the "costs and benefits of alternative actions open to economic agents" (OECD, 1994*b*). They aim to do so by making the environmentally preferred action financially more attractive, relative to its alternatives, than would be the case in a "policy-off" situation.

OECD has actively encouraged the use of economic instruments in environmental policy since the very beginning of its work on environment. It has developed agreed guidelines for the application of economic instruments within Member countries (OECD, 1991*b*), collated information on their use in Member countries (1989, 1994*b*) and analysed their potential and actual application in particular areas, including climate change (1994*c*, 1995*b*, 1996*f*), waste management (1992*a*, *b*), biodiversity (1996*g*) and taxation (1993, 1995*b*, 1996*f*).

Box 6. **Four phases in the evolution of environmental management, as envisaged in the Netherlands**

Phase 1: Company environmental behaviour characterised by: inadequate compliance with environmental regulations, low environmental awareness, little or no organisational provision for environmental protection, protecting the environment regarded as a commercial burden. *Government* relies heavily, if not exclusively, on traditional command and control instruments, *i.e.* detailed permitting systems with provisions for monitoring and fines to encourage compliance.

Phase 2: Company regards compliance with environmental regulations as its primary corporate environmental objective. It will introduce some organisational measures to achieve this objective, environmental awareness is developing slowly, environmental protection is still regarded as something of a business burden but, in general, is accepted and is bearable. *Government* still considers licensing and monitoring to be necessary but the terms of the licence become less detailed in their prescriptive content and greater emphasis is placed on businesses developing their own management systems to assist them in achieving the required outcomes of their licences.

Phase 3: Company compliance with environmental regulations has largely become a matter of course. Environmental awareness is well embedded within the company and its organisational structure and corporate procedures have been further refined to reflect this. In particular, its environmental management system is now well developed. *Government* now feels able to vest a considerable measure of confidence in the company, in relation to its environmental performance, on the basis of the information which the company provides and the sample checks which government agencies undertake. Government responds by making target requirements the heart of its licensing system, simplifying its other requirements, handling licence applications for modifications more flexibly and encouraging a pro-active environmental approach, on the part of the company, to product development.

Phase 4: Government is assured of compliance with environmental regulations through the EMS certificate or Eco-statement. The *Company* regards good environmental performance as an integral corporate objective and is largely self-motivated to focus on continuing product and process environmental improvement. Government can tailor licence and enforcement requirements to the company's environmental management system. The relationship is chiefly based on mutual trust and the company is, *de facto*, largely self-regulating.

Source: Ministry of Housing, Physical Planning and Environment (1995), "Company Environmental Management as a basis for a different relationship between companies and government authorities: A Guide for Government Authorities and Companies", Draft, MHPPE, The Hague (mimeo).

In 1991, the Council of OECD re-confirmed the potential advantages of the use of economic instruments and recommended that Member countries:

i) "make greater and more consistent use of economic instruments as a complement or a substitute to other policy instruments such as regulations, taking into account national socio-economic conditions;

ii) work towards improving the allocation and efficient use of natural and environmental resources by means of economic instruments so as to better reflect the social costs of using these resources;

iii) make efforts to reach further agreement at international level on the use of environmental policy instruments with respect to solving regional or global environmental problems as well as ensuring sustainable development;

iv) develop better modelling, forecasting and monitoring techniques to provide information on environmental consequences of alternative policy actions and their economic effects." (OECD, 1991c).

Most recently, and relating to iv) above, it has carried out an initial evaluation of the efficiency and effectiveness of economic instruments relating to pollution control in Member countries (OECD, 1997b).

Developments in the use of economic instruments

In OECD (1989) a review was presented of the extent of the use of economic instruments in 1987. This covered five categories of instruments: i) charges/taxes, ii) subsidies, iii) deposit-refund systems, iv) market creation instruments and v) financial enforcement incentives – mainly applicable to pollution control and less so to resource pricing and conservation issues. A second survey was conducted in 1992/3 with a narrower coverage of instruments (excluding subsidies, liability and administrative charges) but including a greater number of countries (OECD, 1994b). Subsequently, OECD reviewed the use made of environmentally-related taxes and charges in OECD countries as at the beginning of 1995 (OECD 1996f). Although these studies are not directly comparable, it is possible to derive some general trends from the data.

The 1987 Survey identified 150 instances in 14 OECD countries where "some form of economic arrangement had been made for the sake of improving environmental quality". If subsidies, liability and administrative charges are excluded, the total number of economic instruments is reduced to around 100 or an average of 7 per country surveyed (OECD, 1994b). However, "one finds that in terms of the numbers involved, less than half of the economic instruments reviewed had the intention of generating an economic incentive and over half more meant to raise revenue. Only one third may have effectively had some incentive impact. Basically then, in 1987, environmental policies in the OECD Member countries were command and control policies with some financial and economic add-ons" (OECD, 1994*b*, p. 22).

The 1992/3 survey results suggest a rising trend in the use of economic instruments. Comparing the data for the eight best-documented countries, the number of economic instruments in use in 1992 was 25 per cent higher than in 1987. If the number brought into use in 1993 is also taken into account, the increase is nearly 50 per cent (OECD, 1994*b*). During the period 1987-93, the main increases were in product charges and deposit-refund schemes. The incentive role of economic instruments appears to have become more prominent. In 45 per cent of cases, economic instruments were *intended* to have an incentive effect – "however, the study found little evidence about the existence of incentive effects; in 90 per cent of cases, information on incentive effects was inconclusive or unavailable" (OECD, 1994*b*, p. 13).

An overview of environmentally-related taxes and charges, in use, in OECD countries, as of March 1997, is presented in the OECD publication *Environmental Taxes and Green Tax Reform* (OECD, 1997*d*). The OECD report *Implementation Strategies for Environmental Taxes* concluded that "many existing taxes have been redesigned to reflect better their environmental purpose, and more goods are taxed for environmental purposes" (OECD, 1996*f*).

Two main trends in environmental taxation have been identified over more recent years. One group of countries has radically restructured their tax systems, shifting the tax burden away from income to consumption taxes, including environmental taxes. As a consequence, explicit environmental considerations tend to play a more prominent role in the design of tax reforms in such Member countries as Denmark, Finland, Norway, the Netherlands and Sweden. A second group of Member countries – including Austria, Germany, Hungary, Belgium, France and Switzerland – have made increased use of environmental taxes, both new and existing, but within a narrower framework than one of a comprehensive tax reform.

The use of tradeable permits developed significantly in the United States, in particular in the context of the Acid Rain Program, initiated in 1995. Also, in the field of waste management, deposit-refund systems are increasingly applied and work quite effectively (OECD, 1992*a*, 1994*b*).

In summary, over the period from the mid 1980s to the present, the use of economic instruments in OECD countries has grown significantly, rather than dramatically, and to a varying extent in different Member countries. The impacts which may have resulted are investigated in the next sub-section.

Appraisal and evaluation of economic instruments

The most fully developed and widely applied approach to predicting the benefits from using economic instruments has been by theoretical analysis. Two main types of benefit have been claimed when economic instruments are used in preference to exclusive reliance on command and control systems: static efficiency and dynamic efficiency gains. More recently, a fiscal argument has been added, namely that the introduction of environmental taxes may contribute to the process of fiscal reform and the pursuit of income redistribution objectives.

Typically, *static efficiency gains* are deduced by comparison between the costs incurred under a uniform standards, command and control, scheme and a charges scheme in which dischargers can abate to different levels so that with marginal abatement costs are the same for all dischargers. Empirical studies have estimated the potential cost savings of a variable standards system relative to a uniform standards scheme. These potential cost savings can be very considerable. For example, in a range of US studies which have been reviewed, the bench mark, uniform standards cost was between 0.07 and 21 times higher than the estimated least-cost (Tietenberg, 1990).

However, these theoretically achievable, efficiency gains may not be realised in practice for a number of reasons:

- the "command and control" benchmark may have been wrongly specified (for example, it may have more flexibility than assumed so that strictly uniform standards may not be applied);
- charges may not be set at the appropriate level to achieve the environmental quality target (for example, they may be set at too low a level to have a sufficient incentive effect);
- differences in other costs between the two schemes (*e.g.* set up, administration, monitoring and compliance costs) may require revisions to the above estimates.

Similarly, theoretical analysis has been used to deduce *dynamic efficiency gains* from the use of economic instruments, particularly when they are applied in preference to command and control instruments which restrict the choice of technology. Here, also, the theoretical case may exaggerate the gains which can be achieved in practice:

- not all command and control systems embody such technological rigidities;
- some command and control systems are innovation-forcing;
- economic instruments may not stimulate technical change and innovation if the financial incentives are set at too low a level.

Thus, *ex ante* appraisals, based primarily on theoretical analysis, are no more than suggestive of the types of efficiency gains that *may* be realised in practice. Whether they *are* realised is a matter for *ex post* evaluation to determine. However, it is in this area that empirical analyses are least developed. A recent OECD study has assembled the available evidence relating to the *ex post* evaluation of a number of economic instruments in Denmark, the Netherlands, France, Germany, Sweden, Norway and USA but the findings, though encouraging, remain rather scarce (OECD, 1997*b*).

To a certain extent, this lack of evidence is not surprising, given that the levels of emission charges were, in many cases, believed to be too low to expect a significant effect to occur from this influence alone (OECD, 1996*g*, p. 13). Also, as the study makes clear, *ex post* evaluations of policy instruments frequently forming part of a larger policy package, are inherently complex. A recent OECD study indicates that "In many instances, the case for preferring economic instruments to regulation remains a 'belief' – although it is supported in many cases by *ex ante* quantification and estimates. However, the case for economic instruments is a belief which is not, so far, contradicted by the bulk of the *ex post* evidence described in this report. Whilst the *ex post* evidence available so far cannot conclusively prove the efficiency of economic instruments, it is clear that it would be substantially more difficult to demonstrate the alternative thesis, that regulatory approaches are more efficient than economic instruments." (OECD, 1997*b*). There is, however, growing evidence on the effectiveness of economic instruments, in particular tradeable permits and environmental taxes [Barde and Smith (1997), Barde (1997)].

The income distribution and "double dividend" effects, where environmental taxes and charges form part of a fiscal reform package, have also been subject to some *ex ante* analysis (OECD, 1996*f*, 1997*c*). Income distribution consequences have been most fully examined in the case of proposed carbon taxes and other energy taxes. In a number of instances, these reveal a tendency to regressive income distribution effects, albeit limited. From a policy perspective this could be important:

> "In the first case, there may be policy objectives concerning the position of particular groups, such as the poor and the elderly, which concern policy makers. In the second case; if the gains and losses from environmental tax policies are too unevenly distributed, the losers may form a powerful lobby opposing the introductions of environmental taxes" (OECD, 1996*f*, p. 61).

Hence, a number of environmental tax studies now explore the implications of compensating for these income distribution tendencies through adjustments to other taxes, social security payments etc. within the fiscal system.

A related issue, which has been explored, is the use of environmental tax revenues to finance reductions in taxes on labour in order to promote greater resource efficiency and to increase employment. The majority of the studies suggest modest employment gains may be obtained from this strategy, at least in the short and medium term, but also indicate that the outcome may vary significantly between countries (OECD, 1996f, 1997c).

Whilst these initial evaluation studies of economic instruments have not yet produced definitive findings, they do confirm their potential value, if further developed and applied. As summarised in OECD 1997b, "more evaluation, in short, could contribute to better policy".

2.4 Other instruments

Introduction

These comprise a number of different kinds of instruments, many of which have been introduced into environmental regulatory systems fairly recently or are in the process of being adopted. They may be grouped into three sub-categories:

– environmental planning and environmental assessment instruments;
– voluntary agreements;
– information disclosure schemes and environmental management and audit schemes.

Most of them aim to improve environmental performance by enlisting the voluntary support of the parties involved and supplying them with better information, guidance etc., in order to support achieving environmental objectives in a cost-effective way. They are potentially important measures in the evolution of environmental regulatory systems from traditional command and control systems to predominantly voluntary systems, as illustrated previously in Box 5.

At present, they are mainly used in conjunction with command and control instruments. The command and control system may be retained as a "reserve power", in case the voluntary scheme does not work. Alternatively, voluntary instruments may be used within the command and control system to increase commitment to regulatory objectives and to introduce greater flexibility in the means by which these may be achieved. Because many of these instruments have only been recently implemented, there is only limited evaluation data available.

Environmental planning and environmental assessment instruments

During the first half of the 1990s, national strategic plans on environment and sustainable development have been adopted in a number of Member countries. One of the earliest and most comprehensive of these was the Dutch National Environmental Policy Plan (NEPP), first adopted in 1989 but subsequently up-dated, which identified seven major environmental problems facing the Netherlands, quantified objectives for each to be achieved in years 2000 and 2010, and identified measures by which each of these objectives might be achieved. Typically, these types of plans are indicative but action-oriented; they have a medium term perspective and involve interministerial sharing of responsibilities and partnerships with an array of social actors. They may be complemented by sectoral environmental plans (*e.g.* relating to transport or energy) and more local plans which tend to have a stronger land-use character. Taken together, they can provide an environmental policy and planning framework within which other voluntary instruments, as well as command and control and economic instruments, can be developed and applied in a more focused, complementary and cost-effective manner.

Environmental impact assessment (EIA) procedures have been developed in virtually all OECD countries over the past ten years both to integrate environmental concerns into the planning and design of projects and, subsequently, to enable licensing authorities to take any significant environmental impacts into account in their permitting decisions. Various studies, with some quantitative components, have been undertaken of the practical effects of these procedures, including those associated with the implementation of Directive 85/337/EEC in the Member states of the European Union (Commission of the European Communities, 1993). Although the study findings are not conclusive, the general conclusion is that benefits have exceeded costs, although with the caveat that the net benefit balance could be improved by additional benefit enhancing and cost-effective measures (see CEC, 1993 and Box 7 for further details). The environmental assessment approach is now being extended to sectoral plans, programmes and policies in a number of Member countries. Also, in at least four cases (Canada, Denmark, Netherlands and Portugal) environmental assessment procedures are being used in the environmental appraisal of certain draft bills and draft regulations prior to their adoption.

Life Cycle Analysis (LCA) is a form of analysis which identifies and assesses the likely environmental consequences of a product throughout its life cycle, both upstream (through its earlier stages of production) and downstream (to its eventual disposal as waste). The basic purpose of LCA is to make all of the involved parties (producers, distributors, consumers, NGOs, regulatory bodies) aware of the full environmental costs of specific products and not only those incurred at particular

---

Box 7. **Benefits and costs of EIA procedures**

Relatively few systematic studies have been undertaken of the environmental benefits resulting from the application of EIA procedures. A recent survey of UK studies concluded that a half or more UK projects subject to EIA were modified in an environmentally significant way, that at least a third of these modifications were attributable to the EIA process but that most modifications were of modest rather than major environmental significance.

The main costs of EIA procedures to be considered are of three kinds: the money costs of administering the EIA process, any additional time costs attributable to the process, and any additional mitigation costs due to the process. Typically environmental impact statement (EIS) preparation costs are 0.2 per cent or less of the capital costs of large schemes, rising to around 1 per cent in the case of certain smaller projects. Studies show that the time taken to secure permits can be reduced where the EIA system is functioning well but there is also evidence of delays where there are no clear time limits for the consultation stage or where the authorities are understaffed. Insofar as the EIA process leads to an earlier detection of mitigation requirements, a wider range of mitigation measures may be investigated and a more cost-effective solution found.

Source: Lee, N. (1995), "Environmental Impact Assessment Activities in OECD Countries", Report prepared for OECD Environment Directorate.

---

stages in their life cycles. This information may then be used in different contexts, using a variety of different policy instruments – voluntary, economic and command and control. To date, the main users of LCAs have been firms undertaking them for their own "in-house" purposes, partly to protect their products from market damaging, environmental criticisms. Additionally, a form of life cycle analysis is undertaken for agricultural chemicals in a number of OECD Member countries. The results may be used in making voluntary agreements within producer associations and in the development and application of agricultural chemicals regulations.

A more recent application of LCA techniques is in *Extended Producer Responsibility* (EPR) schemes, which are sometimes called "Shared Product Responsibility (SPR)" schemes (Emery, 1996). A number of OECD countries are seeking to extend private and public sector responsibility for conserving resources and energy and reducing the quantity of pollutants and wastes sent to final disposal. EPR has been defined as a way to "get the price right" by preventing producers from transferring the costs of dealing with the externalities of product systems to other links in the product chain that are less capable of preventing those externalities (OECD, 1996*h*).

Since 1994, OECD has been reviewing the situation in Member countries in what it regards as the "weakest link" in the product responsibility chain – the final disposal of products after their sale to, and use by, consumers. According to the above source, ten OECD governments have adopted national legislation that provides authority to impose EPR requirements on producers of a variety of products and eight other governments have more limited requirements or are envisaging establishing such requirements. However, implementation is only in the early stages. Two illustrations are the Dutch Packaging Covenant (see Box 8 below) and the German Packaging Ordinance.

Voluntary agreements

There are many different kinds of voluntary instruments which range between those where:

a) the parties enter into an informal understanding with government (which may be involved in a consultative or advisory capacity) but where the parties set their own targets and undertake their own monitoring and reporting on the attainment of those targets;

b) the parties enter into a form of contract between government and industry, and negotiate targets with commitments and time schedules on the part of all of the participating parties.

From the perspective of government, the aim is to encourage voluntary action with a desirable social outcome which is to be undertaken by the participant on the basis of his own self interest. This interest may be based on considerations of profit or to reduce the risk of more direct government regulation.

Voluntary instruments take many forms and are known by a variety of different names; for example, covenants, negotiated agreements, self-regulation, codes of conduct, eco-contracts. Although most often applied as means to achieve certain requirements, voluntary agreements can also apply to objectives negotiated between government and industry. Voluntary approaches are hardly ever employed in isolation and, implicitly or explicitly, are often combined with command and control or economic instruments. Typically, voluntary agreements complement existing legislation, *e.g.* 1) when legislation sets performance based objectives, leaving open the ways and means to achieve these objective through some form of voluntary agreement; 2) as experiments or forerunners for future legislation which will be shaped according to the outcome of the voluntary agreement; 3) when there is a common interest within the industry concerned.

They are used in a wide range of countries and are applied to a considerable number of products and technical processes. All indications are that their numbers are increasing. In a recent survey by the International Energy Agency, around 350 different voluntary actions, relevant to energy-related CO_2 abatement, were identified across the OECD area (OECD/IEA, 1996). The majority were characterised as medium/low in terms of legal compulsion; in contrast the Dutch agreements with industry in this area are regarded as highly structured and use rather high compulsion (OECD *Observer*, October/November 1995). Voluntary agreements can take the form of covenants with industry sectors (*e.g.* "accords de branche" in Belgium – Flemish Region). Three voluntary scheme approaches – "the Responsible Care Initiative of the Canadian Chemical Producers Association", the "Dutch Packaging Covenant" and the "OECD Voluntary Industry Commitment on Brominated Flame Retardants" – are illustrated in Box 8.

Yet if voluntary agreements can be a useful and flexible complement to regulations, due consideration must be given to a number of potential pitfalls such as: increased difficulties in monitoring and enforcement, especially when obligations and targets are imprecise or non binding; inadequate sanctions in case of non compliance; possible higher transaction costs; possible reduced confidence of the public; risk of free riding; risk of regulatory capture when industry groups use voluntary agreements to strengthen their market position and exclusion of SMEs from agreements made between the larger companies.

Box 8.   **Three examples of voluntary agreements**

Responsible Care Scheme

This was initiated by the Canadian Chemical Producers Association (CCPA), whose members produce about 90 per cent of chemicals made in Canada, and was developed through six Codes of Practice, between 1986 and 1989. A strong catalyst to its original development was the industry's desire to avoid being subject to stricter regulations by government. The Codes of Practice cover: community awareness and emergency response, research and development, manufacturing, transportation, distribution and hazardous waste management. They commit all members of the CCPA "to achieve a standard of life cycle management of chemicals that meets the public's expectation of responsible environmental performance". They are expected to meet or exceed the letter and spirit of all applicable laws at each stage of operation. A compliance verification process was introduced in 1993.

Each Code of Practice includes criteria for evaluating progress. Implementation and improvement are supervised through six regional leadership groups. The government has not been actively involved in implementation or supervision of the scheme.

(*continued on next page*)

(continued)

However, in recent years, government representations have played some part in consultation groups relating to the Codes of Practice.

The benefits and costs arising from the scheme have not been formally estimated but both business and government have indicated that they regard it as well-designed and successful. It is reported that more than 35 other countries have since instituted similar programmes.

Source: OECD (1996i), *Case Study: Responsible Care Initiative,* Labour Management Programme Meeting, November 1996.

Dutch Packaging Covenant

This was initiated by the Ministry of Housing, Physical Planning and the Environment (VROM) and the Foundation for Packaging and the Environment (FPE) representing packaging manufacturers, packaging users and waste handlers. It has been in existence since 1991 and takes the form of an enforceable covenant. It has a number of quantified objectives to be achieved by year 2000. Annexes to the Covenant contain specific measures that the industry will take to achieve targets. A committee (2 members appointed by the Environment Minister, 2 by industry, with an independent chairman) reviews progress reports submitted by the Foundation.

Preliminary reviews of its operation indicate that the participants in the scheme have considered it useful, although some environmental NGOs are less satisfied. Not much is yet known on the exact benefits and costs of the implementation of the covenant.

Suggestions made for possible improvements include strengthening the connection between the covenant and other environmental policy instruments; and the desirability of addressing the "free rider" problem.

Source: OECD (1996h), *Extended Producer Responsibility in the OECD Area: Phase 1 Report;* F. Neuman (1996), "Extended Producer Responsibility: Case Study of The Dutch Packaging Covenant" (mimeo).

OECD Voluntary Industry Commitment on Brominated Flame Retardants

This was initiated by the major global producers of brominated flame retardants (substances applied to furniture, appliances and textiles to prevent or minimise the occurrence of fires) who committed themselves to take certain actions to reduce the risks posed during the manufacture and disposal of these substances. These actions include such things as committing themselves not to manufacture or import certain individual flame retardants, using best available techniques to improve the purity of others and to minimise levels of releases that occur during manufacture. Beginning in 1998, and every two years thereafter, companies are to report on progress to OECD's policy body on chemical safety. This body will monitor implementation of this action and, if sufficient progress is not made, OECD governments may consider other appropriate actions.

Unfortunately, as yet, there are very few attempts to prepare quantified, *ex post* evaluation studies for voluntary agreements, which can be reported. This is reflected in the more subjective evaluations of voluntary actions for energy-related CO_2 abatement, as illustrated in Box 9. However, some voluntary agreement evaluation studies are now being undertaken which specify criteria and are beginning to apply these, in a preliminary way, using Member country case study data (Storey, 1996).

Information disclosure schemes, environmental audits, environmental management systems and labelling schemes

Information disclosure schemes are provisions, voluntary or mandatory, for enterprises and public authorities to disclose, to the public, information relating to the environmental effects of materials, products and processes under their jurisdiction. This may serve a number of beneficial purposes: encourage enterprises to take voluntary action to reduce their discharges to the environment, enable the public and other interested parties to participate more effectively in consultations prior to the authorisation of new developments, and encourage better enforcement of existing environmental standards and permit conditions.

Box 9.   **Evaluation of voluntary actions for energy-related CO_2 abatement**

- Many officials *feel*... climate change objectives will not be enhanced without an innovative approach such as voluntary actions and co-operative agreements between the public and private sector that go beyond the regulatory process.
- Many officials *believe* that voluntary programmes can achieve energy and environmental objectives faster than regulations because the development of new regulations can take years of research and appraisal.
- There is widespread *belief* that a less confrontational, more interactive approach to achieving energy and environmental policy will bring greater results.
- While not explicitly assessed, many officials *feel* that voluntary programmes might be cheaper to implement than comparable regulatory programmes.
- The question is whether the threat of sanctions is necessary to ensure effectiveness. There is not enough evidence at the present time. Several officials *believe* that effectiveness is not so much a function of sanctions as a function of a "mixed bag" of policy instruments that are used to complement each other and that voluntary programmes should not be used in isolation.

Source: Extracts from "Voluntary Actions for Energy-Related CO_2 Abatement", p. 60 *et seq.* (our emphasis).

Over the past decade, there has been a considerable expansion in public disclosure requirements in OECD countries. In some cases, this has been in response to more general "freedom of information" or "right to know" legislative provisions. In other cases, it has been brought about by modifications to existing command and control systems (*e.g.* extending the "right to know" the terms and conditions of individual permits and monitoring data relating to emissions and environmental quality) or through the information provisions in new legislation (*e.g.* relating to the chemical properties of new products, environmental impact statements or environmental audits). Also, enterprises and authorities are releasing more information on a voluntary basis, recognising that this is more likely to enhance confidence and good will as societies become more open in their behaviour.

In a number of ways OECD Member countries have contributed to these developments. For example, in 1996, an OECD Council Recommendation was negotiated on *Pollutant Release and Transfer Registers*. This recommends to OECD Member governments a set of principles, procedures and actions for government and industry to follow to provide information to the public about sources and potential impacts of industrial pollution. In the same year, OECD published a Guidance Manual for Governments setting down the main considerations to be taken into account in order to realise the benefits of a PRTR while keeping the cost of the system as low as practicable.

With PRTRs in place, governments can better track progress in meeting environmental objectives, and industry can be publicly recognised for doing so. A good case in point is US EPA's "33/50" Programme. In 1991, the US Environmental Protection Agency sent letters to 600 companies which PRTR data showed had the largest total releases of 17 toxic substances. These companies were invited to reduce the emissions in two stages – 33 per cent by 1992 and 50 per cent by 1995 – and report these reductions using the PRTR system. Not only were both goals met ahead of schedule, but EPA saved resources compared to the amount that would have been devoted to regulatory development, and industry was given the flexibility to choose the most cost-effective manner of reducing emissions.

Similarly, Canada introduced a programme in 1991 called ARET (Accelerated Reduction/Elimination of Toxics) which challenges selected Canadian companies, institutions and government facilities to reduce emissions of targeted substances (a 90 per cent reduction of emissions for 30 substances, and a 50 per cent reduction of 87 others, both by the year 2000). Facilities committed to voluntary actions using flexible approaches. As with the 33/50 Programme, progress can be tracked using Canada's PRTR.

Also, a series of Environmental Performance Reviews and State of the Environment reports has facilitated the presentation and analysis of environmental data relating to individual Member countries and the OECD area as a whole. Further, by strengthening provisions for *consultation and public participation* within environmental regulatory frameworks, and supporting *environmental education and training*, Member countries have enhanced the capabilities of the public and consultative organisations to use the available information to greater effect.

Environmental audit and management systems contain provisions, partly statutory and partly voluntary, to review or audit the environmental performance of individual undertakings. Increasingly, audits are being conducted within a structured management system and are integrated within its overall management activity. The purpose of these developments is to enhance the capability of individual undertakings to manage their own environmental affairs, in accordance with well-defined environmental objectives, in an effective and accountable manner.

Environmental auditing was initially developed, in the early 1970s, in the US chemical and oil industries to assure shareholder and others that environmental laws would be respected and that accidents with consequent liabilities were unlikely to occur. During the 1980s, it has progressively spread into other OECD countries and, in 1989, the International Chamber of Commerce (ICC) published its "Guidelines for Environmental Auditing". Increasingly, it is being recognised that environmental auditing procedures need to "nest" within an effective management system. In the United Kingdom, this was initially developed within the environmental management system standard BS7750. In the European Union as a whole an *eco-management and audit scheme* (EMAS) was developed from 1990 onwards and this was finally adopted as Council Regulation 1836/93 in June 1993. An *international standard for environmental management systems* is also being developed in the ISO 14 000 series, which was published in 1996 (see ISO 14001 "Environmental Management Systems – Specification with Guidance for Use"). Participation in these schemes is voluntary but, if choosing to participate, a company must comply with all conditions of the scheme. By mid 1996, approximately 400 sites had been registered under EMAS, of which nearly 300 were located in Germany. It is anticipated that numbers will continue to grow under both the EMAS and ISO 14 001 schemes, with "bridging" arrangements established between the two. A significant and growing number of other organisations, including municipalities, are now developing their own auditing and environmental management systems.

Environmental labelling schemes now exist in many OECD countries, for example "Environmental Choice" in Canada, "Blue Angel" in Germany, "Eco-mark" in Japan, (OECD, 1995c). Participation in these schemes is voluntary (sometimes at the initiative of the private sector, *e.g.* the "Green Seal" in the United States) but approval to use the environmental label is usually made by an official committee or independent expert group.

2.5 Overall impacts of environmental regulatory reform

It is apparent, from the preceding review of specific environmental regulatory reforms that, for the most part, quantified estimates of their respective benefits and costs are not available. The same is broadly true when considering the benefits and costs of environmental regulatory reforms as a whole. However, because of periodic concerns about the overall effectiveness of environmental protection policies and their economic consequences, some studies have been carried out which have attempted to review their overall consequences. These are briefly reviewed below.

Pollution abatement and control (PAC) *expenditures* by the public and private sectors have, according to OECD surveys covering a number of Member countries, probably increased somewhat more than GDP over this period. However, the increase is from a relatively low base-line, reaching between 1 per cent and 2 per cent of GDP by the mid 1990s in those Member countries for which data are available (OECD SIREN Data-Base 1995).

Economy-wide and employment effects of existing and potential environmental policies, covering both environmental regulation and expenditures, have been examined in a number of studies (for example, OECD, 1997c, DRI, 1994). Additionally, a study has been undertaken by the OECD Economics Department, on the economy-wide effects of regulatory reform, for the Regulatory Reform Review but this specifically excluded consideration of environmental, health and safety regulations. Also, the methodology used, based on a particular approach to bench-marking, means that its findings are not directly comparable with those of the above studies.

The overall conclusion reached in the *Environmental Policies and Employment* report (OECD, 1997c), which is based on a number of modelling and other studies, is:

- the employment effects of environmental policies appear to be small, relative to total employment levels, and tend to be swamped by other, more influential changes taking place in the economy; and
- if anything, environmental policies have had a small net beneficial effect on employment, at least in the short and medium term.

This does not imply that adverse employment effects do not result from environmental regulatory changes in particular industrial sectors or localities, nor that there is no scope to improve the cost-effectiveness and economic benefits of environmental policies. For example, the DRI study focused on the environmental and economic benefits which could result from a more integrated approach to the future development of environmental and economic policies (DRI, 1994).

The effect of environmental regulation on *innovation and productivity* continues to be an area of dispute. Repetto et al. (1996) have challenged the view that environmental protection has reduced productivity growth. They argue that the measures used have failed to take account, in the output measure, of the environmental improvements that protection measures have achieved. They also present corrected measures in support of their argument. Similarly, Porter and Van der Linden (1995) argue, on the basis of case study evidence, that well-designed environmental regulations can stimulate innovation and enhance competitiveness. However, this has been challenged by Palmer *et al.* (1995). A fuller review of the recent literature is contained in OECD (1996*k*) and confirms that the findings on the net costs and benefits of environmental regulation, in terms of its effect on productivity, are varied and conflicting.

The OECD Committee on Competition Law and Policy has recently reviewed various modes of environmental regulation in an attempt to identify any *anti-competition effects* which can accompany them (OECD, 1996*l*,). The accompanying Note, prepared by the Secretariat, states:

"The common denominator among the various modes of intervention [...] is that the polluter pays, that producers and consumers must bear the full social costs of their actions. It implies that when production has harmful effects on the environment, those effects must be reflected in costs, allowing the price mechanism to perform its role as an indicator. This principle in itself is consistent with competition policy to the extent that it remedies a market failure, internalising the pollution externality" (*op. cit.*, 1996*l*, p. 5).

The report contains a number of case studies which illustrate how different types of environmental regulations, including voluntary agreements, may contain anti-competitive features. Whilst there is no evidence presented to suggest that these are pervasive or serious, nonetheless they are proper subjects for evaluation within a systematic, environmental regulatory reform process.

Similar conclusions apply when considering the effects of environmental regulations on *international trade*, that is, internalising environmental externalities to combat the adverse consequences of market failure should not, of itself, be regarded as a distorting influence on international trade (OECD, 1994*d*).

Overall, there is a short-fall of convincing evidence that environmental regulations have had a significant negative effect on economic performance, despite fears expressed that this may be the case. Furthermore these assessments do not take into account the *benefits* provided by environmental regulation and policies. This does not deny scope for potential improvements in cost-effectiveness, environmental effectiveness and distributional effects to which strengthened appraisal/evaluation procedures could usefully contribute.

2.6 Linkages between ERR and RR in overall appraisal

The review, so far, has been largely confined to the environmental consequences and economic consequences of the existing environmental regulatory system and its reform (ERR), that is, to "A" and "B" consequences in Figure 1 (see Section 1.3).

The economic consequences of the economic regulatory system and its reform, (*i.e.* of "C" consequences in Figure 1), is the central focus of the general regulatory reform (RR) study which is being concurrently, but separately, undertaken. Therefore, from an ERR perspective, the issue arises as to how the environmental consequences of economic RR ("D" consequences in Figure 1), the relationship between environmental and economic regulatory systems ("E") and between environmental and economic consequences ("F") are being considered within the overall RR process.

The RR Work Plan (OECD, 1996*a*) has provided for the preparation of:

– six sectoral studies: telecommunications; professional services; electricity; financial services; agro-food and product standards; and

– five thematic reports: economy-wide effects of regulatory reform; competition, consumers and regulatory reform; industrial competitiveness, innovation and regulatory reform; market openness and regulatory reform; and reform of the public sector to carry out and sustain regulatory reform.

The *agro-food study* includes a brief qualitative examination of the possible adverse effects of environmental regulations on the economic performance of the agro-food industry ("B" consequences) and of agricultural subsidies on environmental quality ("D" consequences) (OECD, 1996*m*). There is also an implicit recognition of "E" type consequences but this is not developed. The *product standards report* mainly addresses the impact of product standards on international trade, competition and innovation and suggests, in its executive summary, that where certain standards are "excessively restrictive" the impact can be "particularly serious" (OECD, 1996*n*). However, there is no specific examination of the environmental issues which are involved, although consideration is given to wider issues of product safety.

The *electricity* study explores certain of the relationships, identified in Figure 1, between electricity sector reform and its environmental consequences. It notes that the power sector has a very significant effect on the environment and that the environmental consequences of its reform ("D" consequences) may be positive or negative according to the circumstances of the particular case. It also acknowledges that some adjustments to environmental regulation may be needed to compensate for the market's inability to internalise all of its environmental externalities (*i.e.* to take account of "E" consequences). The report also explores various environmental and economic consequences (in "A", "B", "C" and "D" categories) of energy subsidies, energy taxes and tradeable emission permits. However, for the most part, the analysis is fairly brief and qualitative and the outcomes, in a number of cases, are uncertain (OECD, 1997*e*).

As previously stated, the report on *economy-wide effect of regulatory reform* excludes environmental, health and safety regulations from its terms of reference and, in effect, focuses on the economic and social consequences associated with economic regulations (although, certain of the sectors which it covers, for example, electricity generation and transmission, and airlines and road transport, are often associated with significant environmental impacts) (OECD, 1996*j*). The report *on regulatory reform, industrial competitiveness and innovation* refers to social regulation, including environmental regulation, as well as to economic regulation (OECD, 1996*k*). It notes that, in all domains, regulatory reform should be based on a comparison of costs and benefits. However, most published studies do not take into account the benefits that may be associated with regulatory policies, particularly social regulations such as environmental protection (p. 6). Its survey of the existing literature relating to regulatory reform (environmental and other forms), and its effect on productivity, is therefore largely confined to the economic impact of environmental and economic regulation ("B" and "C" consequences). The report on *regulatory quality and public sector reform* acknowledges, as does the previously mentioned report, differences in character between economic and social/ environmental regulatory reform and the common need to base these on benefit-cost criteria (OECD, 1997*a*). However, the main focus of the report is on economic regulatory reform and their economic consequences.

Thus, it appears that "D", "E" and "F" consequences are incompletely covered in the RR studies and, in particular, linkages between the reform of the general regulatory system and of the environmental regulatory system are relatively neglected.

The OECD Council meeting, in May 1995, requested OECD "to pursue the integration of environmental with economic and other policies" as well as to "pursue regulatory reform." (OECD, 1996*a*, p. 3). Significant progress has been made, through a number of OECD studies, undertaken during the first half of the 1990s, to develop understanding of the policy linkages between the environmental sector on the one hand and the transport, energy, agriculture and trade sectors on the other (OECD, 1996o). Logically, this understanding should be carried over into the regulatory reform process which would imply giving further consideration to:

- whether certain economic regulatory reforms (*e.g.* de-regulation, privatisation, trade liberalisation measures) have any consequential effects on the efficiency and effectiveness of environmental regulatory systems;
- whether some economic regulatory reforms (*e.g.* structural adjustment programmes supported by overseas aid) have indirect environmental consequences resulting from the economic and social changes they bring about;
- whether other economic regulatory reforms (*e.g.* liberalising access to and usage of natural resources) have indirect economic consequences via the environmental changes they bring about; and
- whether environmental regulatory reforms have equivalent kinds of indirect consequences (negative or positive) on economic performance and environmental quality.

Section 3

THE ROLE OF REGULATORY IMPACT ANALYSIS IN ENVIRONMENTAL REGULATORY REFORM

3.1 Introduction

For the purposes of this report, *regulatory impact analysis* (RIA) includes both regulatory appraisal and regulatory evaluation. *Regulatory appraisal* is used to describe the *ex ante* assessment of proposed new or revised regulations, whereas *regulatory evaluation* refers to the *ex post* assessment of existing regulations. Evaluation may be undertaken either for the environmental regulatory system as a whole or for individual regulatory instruments.

In 1995, the Council of the OECD recommended that Member countries should take measures to secure the quality of government regulations by systematically examining their quality and performance, according to certain criteria (see Box 10).

**Box 10.   OECD Council Recommendation on Improving
the Quality of Government Regulation**

In 1995, the Council of the OECD adopted a Recommendation which, *inter alia,*

"Recommends that Member countries take effective measures to ensure the quality and transparency of government regulations by steps such as:

i) examining the quality and performance of administrative and political processes for developing, implementing, evaluating, and revising regulations, using as a guide the principles set out in The Reference Check-List for Regulatory Decision-Making..."

Included within the Check-List are the following criteria:

● "Regulators should routinely *estimate the total expected costs and benefits* of each regulatory proposal and of feasible alternatives, and should make the estimates available in accessible format to administrative and political decision-makers"(§30).

(continued on next page)

(continued)

- "Government should take a pragmatic and realistic approach to this issue...Qualitative assessments may be a useful beginning where analytical skills are low, where the cost of information collection is high, or where there is little consensus on how to value benefits." (§31).

- "To the extent that distributive and equity values are affected by government intervention, regulators should make transparent the *distribution of regulatory costs and benefits across social groups*" (§33).

- "Regulations should be developed in an *open and transparent* fashion, with appropriate procedures for *effective* and *timely input from interested parties* such as affected businesses and trade unions, other interest groups, or other levels of government" (§35).

Source: OECD, 1995*a*, "Recommendations of the Council of the OECD on Improving the Quality of Government Regulation" (Adopted on 9th March 1995).

Regulatory appraisal and evaluation already exist, in some form, in all Member countries. However, this review is confined primarily to those situations where it is undertaken as a *formalised, structured requirement,* either on a continuing or periodic basis.

The purpose and content of regulatory reviews vary considerably according to the policy agendas of governments:

"Some countries assess business impacts, other, administrative and paperwork burdens. Others used full-fledged benefit-cost analysis based on social welfare theories. Environmental impact assessment is used to identify potential impacts of regulations on environmental quality. Other regulators assess how proposed rules affect sub-national governments, or aboriginal groups, or small businesses, or international trade." (OECD, 1996*p*; Note by PMS secretariat for Meeting on Regulatory Impact Analysis, May 1996).

The different types of appraisals and evaluations of environmental regulations which are being conducted in OECD countries are reviewed below. Particular attention is paid to those which assess performance in terms of *overall efficiency,* including *environmental* and *cost-effectiveness,* and *distributional consequences.* The review is based upon literature and experience relating specifically to *environmental regulatory systems* and more general literature relating to *regulatory reform management* and *regulatory impact analysis.*

3.2 Current status of regulatory impact analysis

The Environment Directorate's Questionnaire Survey on Environmental Regulatory Reform obtained information from responding Member countries on their use of formalised appraisal and evaluation measures relating to environmental regulations (Environment Directorate, 1996). Based on this source, it would appear that the following have some such measures in place: Belgium, Canada, Denmark, European Commission, Hungary, Mexico, Netherlands, Norway, Portugal, Spain, Sweden, Turkey, United Kingdom and the United States. Additionally, from the Public Management Service's surveys of RIA in OECD countries, it is possible to identify a number of other Member countries which use RIA for more general regulatory review purposes, and which probably include the review of environmental regulations (OECD, 1997*a* and 1997*f*). These countries include Australia, Austria, Finland, Italy, Japan and New Zealand.

The overall trend is one of increased adoption and use of formalised RIA over time. However, the types of information used and its analytical and procedural requirements, as well as the extent of its application, are quite variable between countries, as illustrated below.

An important distinguishing feature, when classifying RIA instruments, is the appraisal or evaluation criteria and methods which they use. Several methods can be used: multi-criteria analysis, subjective scoring methods, risk-benefit analysis, impact evaluation, cost-effectiveness analysis. The most comprehensive instruments are those which use some form of *cost-benefit* framework. However, the costs and benefits (especially benefits) may be appraised in different ways, ranging from a qualitative or judgmental assessment to formalised cost-benefit analyses requiring sophisticated evaluation methods; but the latter approach may be too complex, costly or lengthy to apply in certain cases. A *distributive* criterion can be added or, alternatively, the cost-benefit criterion may be decomposed into *cost-effectiveness* and *environmental effectiveness* measures. In other cases, the criteria may focus more narrowly on *cost-effectiveness* for one constituent group within a country – for example, *regulatory compliance costs* for the business sector or *fiscal implications* for the government sector, or *trade and competitiveness* implications.

The different types of RIA employed in OECD Member countries, according to the above criteria, are shown in Table 3. Variants on the cost-benefit criterion appear to be used in nine of these cases: Australia, Canada, Denmark, European Commission, Finland, Mexico, Norway, UK, and USA. However, they are not used in all situations in these countries, nor is a formalised, monetary CBA usually undertaken. More frequently, cost-only criteria appear to be used either in the form of business-cost, or public sector/national budget, indicators.

Table 1. **Appraisal and evaluation methods applied to environmental regulations in OECD Member countries**

COUNTRY	METHODS USED
Australia	Benefit/cost analysis applied to bills and lower-level rules that may have significant business/cost impacts (applied at Commonwealth and certain state levels).
Austria	Fiscal analysis recommended for bills.
Canada	Benefit/cost analysis (with findings presented in a Regulatory Impact Analysis Statement) supplemented by Business Impact Test and Regulatory Cost Account Protocol.
Denmark	General impact analysis required for new legal proposals which, inter alia, may require both an economic study and an environmental impact assessment.
European Union	Treaty on European Union (article 130 r. 3) requires that the costs and benefits of each proposed regulatory action be assessed.
Finland	General impact analysis, distributional and fiscal analyses applied to bills and lower-level rules.
Hungary	The Act on Environment prescribes detailed economic evaluations of proposed environmental regulations.
Italy	"Cost-output analysis" used, with the main emphasis placed on fiscal costs.
Japan	General impact analysis applied, as necessary, to permit rules and social regulations.
Mexico	Cost-benefit and cost-effectiveness analyses applied to "business-related" procedures and requirements.
Netherlands	General impact analysis for bills and lower-level rules. Regulatory impact analyses of likely financial effects of new regulations on industry and trade. RIAs may also cover environmental impact assessments of proposed regulatory changes originating from non-environment Ministries.
New Zealand	Fiscal analysis/compliance cost assessment applied to draft laws originating from Cabinet.
Norway	Studies of economic impacts of proposed regulations, sometimes in the form of cost-benefit analyses. Also review undertaken of the effects of environmental policy instruments in relation to goal achievement, cost-effectiveness, distributional effects and effects on technological development.
Portugal	Fiscal analysis of bills and lower-level rules; also environmental impact assessment of certain bills.
Spain	Financial analysis of effect of regulatory proposals on public budget.

(continued on next page)

(continued)	
Turkey	General impact analysis for bills and lower-level regulations.
United Kingdom	Compliance Cost Assessment of new and amended regulations, focusing particularly on costs to business. A fuller cost-benefit analysis may be undertaken in certain cases.
United States	Regulatory analysis has evolved from a relatively simple analysis of costs to a comprehensive benefit-cost analysis for actions subject to Executive Order 12866. In other contexts, EPA also carries out Regulatory Flexibility Analyses and more specific cost and cost-benefit analyses in accordance with the Clean Water and Clean Air Acts.
Sources:	Environment Directorate (1996); OECD (1996*p*), "An Overview of Regulatory Impact Analysis in OECD Countries"; OECD (1997*a*), "Regulatory Quality and Public Sector Reform".

Other similarities and differences between RIAs in use in different Member countries are summarised below:

- Most RIAs relate to the *appraisal of proposed new regulations* and are intended to inform decisions concerning their approval. Relatively few are being used in the *evaluation of existing regulations*, particularly covering the entire environmental regulatory system or a substantial part of it. Where such evaluations do take place, they are more likely to be undertaken on a "one off" basis rather than as part of a continuing regulatory reform management programme.

- Certain of the RIAs have a well-defined methodology which is specified in guidance documents or manuals. A number of those in use in seven Member countries (Australia, Canada, the Netherlands, Norway, Sweden, United Kingdom and the United States) are described and analysed in Hopkins (1996). The documentation covers, *inter alia*: the scope and status of the RIA; the type of analysis and methodology it uses; its data requirements; who does the analysis and what quality controls exist; who uses the analysis and in what ways; and provisions for public access and disclosure. Comparable information is not available for other RIAs but it is believed to be less developed and/or accessible elsewhere.

- The provisions made for consultation, particularly public consultation, during regulatory appraisal and evaluation are quite variable. A recent study of the role of public consultation within general regulatory reform procedures in ten Member countries found that the greatest use was still made of such traditional consultative methods as "advisory bodies" and "informal consultation" (OECD, 1997*a*). However, the study also noted a trend towards more open decision making, the establishment of more formalised provisions for public consultation and greater opportunities for the public and other interested parties to obtain draft RIA documentation for comment. The extent of public disclosure of the findings of regulatory appraisals is also variable. According to the Environment Directorate's survey, some provisions for this (in certain cases, in summary form) exist in Australia, Canada, the Netherlands, Sweden, the United Kingdom and the United States (Environment Directorate, 1996).

● The provisions made for quality control of regulatory impact analysis and, more generally, of the regulatory reform process as a whole, differ between Member countries. One principal distinction is between those RIAs where quality control is exercised internally by the regulators involved and where there is some measure of external review, either involving another section of the government administration or through outside peer review. Different forms of external review have been recorded, *inter alia*, in the case of Australia, Canada, the Netherlands, Sweden, the United Kingdom, and the United

---

Box 11. An overview of two decades' experience of RIA

"Assessments of the results of two decades of investment in RIA show a very mixed picture. On one hand, there is nearly universal agreement among regulatory reform offices that RIA, when it is done well, improves the costs-effectiveness of regulatory decisions. In 1987, for example, the USEPA evaluated fifteen RIAs and found that they cost $10 million to conduct but resulted in revisions to regulations with estimated net benefits of about $10 billion.

Yet positive views are balanced by evidence of massive non-compliance and quality problems. A recent survey of benefit-cost analyses in the United States found that half of the adopted regulations did not pass a benefit-cost test, even after fifteen years of investment in a benefit-cost programme.* In 1992, an Australian official (in an interview with the OECD Secretariat) listed several problems that he considered existed in the federal RIA programme:

'Quality varies enormously. Assertions are often not well-supported. Little assessment of benefits is the most common failing. The statement of purpose is often inadequate. We have real problems getting departments to apply welfare economics analysis to benefit-cost type judgements. The Regulatory Impact Statement (RIS) often becomes a justification for what they want to do any way.'"

---

* Hahn, R., 1996, "Regulatory Reform: What Do the Government's Numbers Tell Us?", Conference Paper, American Enterprise Institute, Washington DC.

Source: OECD, 1997*a*, p. 7 *et seq.*

States (OECD, 1997*a*). The trend towards greater external involvement in RIA control appears to be continuing.

Insufficient is yet known about the practical effects of developing and applying RIA instruments in Member countries, both in the context of general regulatory reform and, more particularly, of environmental regulatory reform. However, the available information suggests that *a*) where RIA works satisfactorily and effectively, it can be a very cost-effective tool which also yields additional benefits but *b*) quality problems and non-compliance problems are still widespread, as illustrated in Box 11. The possible causes of these, as identified in OECD, 1997*a*, are shown in Box 12.

3.3 OECD appraisal and evaluation studies

The foregoing review indicates a continuing need to strengthen regulatory impact analysis as an integral element of the ERR process.

At its meeting, in January 1991, the Council of the OECD recommended that Member countries should "develop better modelling, forecasting and monitoring techniques to provide information on environmental consequences of alternative policy actions and their economic effects". In response to this, in 1996, the Group on Economic and Environment Policy Integration completed the study *Evaluating Economic Instruments for Environmental Policy* (OECD, 1997*b*). The contents of this report are likely to be of general methodological interest to the ERR process:

- it reviews the advantages and shortcomings of evaluation studies of environmental interest from the different perspectives – theoretical and empirical, *ex ante* and *ex post* – from which they may be undertaken;

- it identifies the criteria by which evaluations might be undertaken within a broad cost-benefit framework, including environmental effectiveness, cost-effectiveness, indirect linkage effects and distributional considerations;

- it evaluates, in a preliminary manner and on the basis of the data available, a range of economic instruments of environmental policy which are currently in use in Member countries;

- it examines the institutional context of evaluation studies and proposes an "in-built" evaluation procedure for future use. This procedure is intended to commence during the conceptualisation and design of the policy instrument and continue during its subsequent adaptation, implementation and enforcement (OECD, 1997*b*).

Box 12. **Possible causes of quality and non-compliance problems with RIA**

1. **Technical features**

    Some analytical techniques, particularly for cost-benefit analysis, are not suffi-ciently developed. Methods for developing and using qualitative analysis need more attention.

2. **Value conflicts and power struggles**

    Resistance may be high since some interest groups and regulators consider RIA as contrary to their ethos.

    Interest groups who benefit from the use of other decision methods feel threatened.

3. **Institutional and resource issues**

    Inadequate incentives for regulators to use RIAs. Sanctions for non-compliance are inadequate in some countries.

    Inadequate regulatory capacity to comply, given lack of skills or resources.

4. **Legal issues**

    Laws may require regulators to pursue their regulatory missions irrespective of cost and, therefore, do not allow for the balancing of benefits and costs or for trade-offs.

5. **Practical issues**

    Quality control is often poor, reducing the benefits of RIA.

    RIAs may be prepared too late in the regulatory process, after key decisions have been taken.

    Regulators are under pressure to make decisions quickly – analysis and consultation can slow down the process.

6. **Political issues**

    RIA may supply some information which is not in demand from politicians who may wish to focus on narrower interests rather than include wider and more diffuse interests in their considerations.

Source: OECD (1996p), p. 8.

Whilst recognising the difficulties in carrying out good quality evaluation studies, nevertheless the study concludes:

"This report has shown that evaluations of actual practice in using eco-nomic instruments in environmental policy can shed valuable light on the efficiency and effectiveness of environmental policy. Ex *post* evaluation of actual practice can provide a valuable supplement to what is already known from theoretical arguments and simulation studies about the advantages and disadvantages of such instruments [...] More evaluation, in short, could contribute to better policy" (OECD, 1997*b*).

"[...] there would also be benefits from wider evaluation of the performance of environmental policy measures more generally. The costs and benefits of all forms of environmental policy measures could be evaluated along the lines suggested here. [...] It would, for example, be desirable to look much more closely and systematically than has been the practice up to now at the performance in practice of regulatory policies, using an administrative rather than an incentive approach to pollution control [...] It is clear that a similar test, based on performance evidence, needs also to be addressed to the alternative approaches or policy packages available in environmental policy." (OECD, 1997*b*).

Box 13. **An overall strategy for improving regulatory quality**

A. **Building a *Regulatory Management System***

   1. Adopt a regulatory reform policy at the highest political levels.
   2. Establish explicit standards for regulatory quality and principles of regulatory decision-making.
   3. Build up central, and other, management capacities for regulatory reform and improving regulatory quality.

B. **Improving the Quality of New Regulations**

   1. Develop and apply appropriate regulatory appraisal methods.
   2. Systematise public consultation procedures and other (external) procedures for quality control.
   3. Consider using alternatives to formal, direct regulation.
   4. Improve regulatory co-ordination.

C. **Upgrading the Quality of Existing Regulation**

   1. Develop and apply appropriate regulatory evaluation methods.
   2. Systematise public consultation procedures and other quality control procedures.
   3. Improve regulatory co-ordination.

Source: Adapted from OECD, 1997*a*, p. 21.

A similar approach, based on the same evaluation criteria, has also been used in an initial evaluation of a number of voluntary agreements, designed to improve energy efficiency and reduce greenhouse gas emissions, in different Member countries (Storey, 1996).

Parallel to these studies, there have been a greater number of other studies under the supervision of OECD's Public Management Service, relating to regulatory impact analysis and its role in the general regulatory reform process. Certain of these are relevant to appraisal and evaluation activities within the ERR process.

In particular, these studies highlight the need, if regulatory reform is to be successful, to integrate regulatory impact analysis within a broader-based strategy for improving regulatory quality. This strategy, as illustrated in Box 13, should include provisions for strengthening management capacity for regulatory reform. Improving the quality of RIAs and their effectiveness within the ERR process will require more than technical improvements to methods of appraisal and evaluation and the provision of better quality data.

Section 4

CONCLUSIONS AND RECOMMENDATIONS

4.1 Introduction

This report has reviewed the objectives of, and progress in, environmental regulatory reform (ERR) within OECD countries, principally over the past decade. It has adopted a broad definition of the environmental regulatory system to include not only "command and control" measures but also economic and planning instruments and voluntary agreements. It has also taken account of the linkages between environmental and other sectoral regulatory activities (see Figure 1 in Section 1.3).

Various surveys have shown that the preceding ten years have witnessed considerable environmental regulatory change and reform. This has been driven as much by changing regulatory requirements (due to economic growth, structural and institutional change, trends towards globalisation and regulatory decentralisation) as by an intensification of regulatory reform pressures. In turn, these developments have been accompanied by the widening application of regulatory impact analysis (RIA) techniques. However, despite these advances and the benefits which have flowed from them, the size and complexity of the environmental tasks to be addressed by regulatory systems has continued to grow and the mechanisms to address these require further strengthening by means other than their automatic expansion and elaboration.

This final chapter summarises the main findings of the review and makes suggestions on how to strengthen the ERR process and make it more adaptive to continuing economic, technical and institutional change.

4.2 The case for ERR restated

The need for environmental regulation arises from the emergence of environmental externalities which result from *market failures*. The need for ERR arises from the emergence of *regulatory failures i.e.* deficiencies in dealing satisfactorily with externalities within the regulatory system (Section 1.2).

Regulatory deficiencies cannot always be remedied by simple means. For example, deregulation, by itself, is not a solution unless it is capable of recreating perfectly competitive market conditions. Nor, according to second best theory, does deregulation, by itself, necessarily reduce environmental problems by creating more (but imperfect) competition.

The central questions to be considered in the ERR process, as illustrated in Box 3 in Section 1.2, are:

-   can the costs of existing and proposed regulations be justified by the benefits to which they give rise, and

-   are the regulatory interventions, which are under consideration, expected to give rise to greater net benefits than alternative regulatory measures?

-   Other criteria include: administration and compliance costs, wider economic effects (effects on price level, technical innovation, employment, trade), distributive implications (*e.g.* on income groups, industries, regions), capacity building.

This test is applicable to existing regulations, changes to these through deregulation or regulatory revision, and to proposals for new regulations. Similarly, it applies equally to general regulatory systems and their reform as it does to the environmental regulatory system and its reform.

The ERR process should consider the benefits *and* costs, environmental *and* economic, of existing regulatory systems and proposed changes to these, as well as their distributional consequences. Similarly, the cost-benefit rationale should be central to any *regulatory impact analyses* (RIAs) which help to guide the ERR process.

4.3 Progress in implementing ERR

ERR is under way in virtually all of the Member countries which responded to the Environment Directorate's Questionnaire on Regulatory Reform (Section 2.1). It is being driven by a combination of initiatives within environmental ministries and more general regulatory reform initiatives from within other ministries of Member country governments. In the latter case, the stronger motivation is often to improve overall economic performance by increasing competitiveness, stimulating technical progress and promoting international trade and, thereby, attempting to increase economic growth and reduce unemployment. In the former case, a stronger initial consideration may be to improve the effectiveness of environmental regulation though, increasingly, this is tempered by the same range of economic considerations as mentioned above.

All environmental regulatory systems are, to a significant degree, hybrid systems comprising a collection of command and control instruments, supplemented by a number of economic and planning instruments and voluntary agreements (Section 2.1). Most of these have experienced considerable change over the last decade. In virtually all cases, command and control instruments remain the major constituent but this belies the extent to which innovation has taken place both within the command and control sub-system and through the development of other complementary environmental policy instruments.

Command and control instruments. The main types of reforms which have taken place within this sub-system include: simplification of bureaucratic procedures and paper work; greater flexibility in choosing the best means of achieving environmental standards; the progressive adoption of integrated permitting schemes; the integration of environmental impact assessment (EIA) procedures in mandatory permitting and planning procedures; the setting of time limits for consultation and public participation; and the greater use of permit charges and compliance fines to support more effective regulatory activities and to help in addressing problems of non-compliance (Section 2.2). However, the practical consequences of these reforms have not yet been quantified in most cases, although their effects are broadly believed to be beneficial.

Economic instruments. These are broadly defined to include environmental charges and taxes, deposit-refund systems, market creation instruments, financial enforcement incentives and abatement subsidies. Studies covering the first three categories of economic instruments indicate that a significant increase has occurred in the numbers and types of these instruments in use within the OECD area. Also, their incentive effect, which was relatively weak a decade ago because of the relatively low level at which many of these financial measures were set, has improved over more recent years. An initial evaluation of the effects of the use of these economic instruments is broadly positive in its findings although, due to data deficiencies and for methodological reasons, the conclusions are largely qualitative and conditional (Section 2.3).

Other instruments. These comprise a diverse group of planning-related instruments, voluntary agreements, information schemes and environmental management and audit systems whose development and growth, over the most recent years, have been substantial. A *priori*, theoretical appraisals have identified a range of potentially beneficial environmental and economic benefits from their use. However, partly because a number of them have only been recently introduced and partly because regulatory impact analyses have not been widely developed and applied to this range of instruments, quantitative evidence of their effects is limited.

Where it does exist, for example in relation to environmental impact assessment procedures, the findings are positive but suggest that the full potential benefits are not yet being realised (Section 2.4).

4.4 Overall effects of ERR

In common with the case of general regulatory reform, quantitative evidence relating to the costs and benefits of existing and proposed environmental regulatory instruments is very incomplete. However, some broad-based information is available concerning certain of the items that would be included in overall cost-benefit studies of environmental regulatory systems. These support the view that:

–   significant environmental benefits have resulted from the application of existing and reformed environmental regulatory systems in Member countries; and

–   contrary to some opinions, the costs associated with their implementation have, so far, not had significant adverse economic consequences – on the contrary, in certain circumstances, they may have been marginally beneficial (Section 2.5).

However, the findings provide no cause for complacency. There is sufficient qualitative and other circumstantial evidence to suggest that there is scope for further improvements in environmental and cost-effectiveness, and in the distributional consequences, of existing environmental regulatory systems. This can only be confirmed, and its nature and extent better defined, after more systematic regulatory impact analyses have been completed. Also, most existing studies have not adequately examined the linkages between environmental and general regulatory systems and the interactive consequences of reforms, existing and envisaged, of each. Until this is undertaken, the regulatory impact picture will remain incomplete.

4.5 Regulatory impact analysis and regulatory reform strategies

Regulatory impact analysis (RIA) of environmental regulations, whether in the form of *ex ante* appraisal or *ex post* evaluation, exists in some form in a significant and growing number of Member countries (see Table 3). However, the *type* of RIA which is used, and the *extent* to which it is procedurally and methodologically developed, is highly variable, as indicated below.

- Some form of *cost-benefit* criterion is used in a significant and growing number of cases. In certain of these, the coverage of impacts is not comprehensive and a mixture of qualitative and quantitative information is used. In other cases, cost-effectiveness, environmental effectiveness, regulatory compliance cost, fiscal analysis or distributive analysis may be used as performance criteria, either separately or in different combinations.

- More RIAs relate to *new regulations* than to existing regulatory systems.

- Well developed *methodologies and guidance materials* have been prepared for some RIA procedures but do not exist, or are not readily available, in other cases.

- Provisions for *consultation and public participation* during the RIA process, and for public disclosure of RIA documentation and findings, are very variable. Where they exist, the traditional consultation methods of informal consultation and use of advisory bodies are more widely used.

- Provisions for *quality control* in undertaking RIAs, and in their effective use for regulatory reform, are also variable. In many cases, quality control appears to be exercised by the regulators themselves, but the extent of external involvement in quality control seems to be growing, although from a low base-line.

- Available evidence on RIA *practice* is limited but suggests *a*) where it has been satisfactorily applied, it has yielded substantial cost savings and other benefits but *b*) quality problems and compliance problems are quite widespread and, therefore, practice is likely to fall below potential (Section 3.2).

OECD initiatives, both in relation to environmental regulatory reform and more general regulatory reform, have encouraged the more effective development and application of RIA procedures, over recent years (Section 3.3). The Council Meeting of Environmental Ministers, in January 1991, recommended that Member countries should "develop better modelling, forecasting and monitoring techniques to provide information on the environmental consequences of alternative policy actions and their economic effects". In response to this, two evaluation studies, based on a cost-benefit rationale and relating to the use of economic instruments and voluntary agreements, were completed in 1996. In the first of these, the Group on Economic and Environmental Policy Integration concluded:

"Evaluation of actual practice in using economic instruments in environmental policy can shed valuable light on the efficiency and effectiveness of environmental policy.

It is clear that a similar test, based on performance evidence, needs also to be addressed to the alternative approaches or policy packages available in environmental policy" (OECD, 1996*g*, p. 140).

Furthermore, in 1995, the Council of the OECD, in its "Recommendation on Improving the Quality of Government Regulation", indicated that Regulators should:

- Estimate the total expected costs and benefits of each regulatory proposal and of feasible alternatives, and make the estimates available to decision-makers.

- Make transparent the distribution of regulatory costs and benefits across social groups.

- Develop regulations in an open and timely fashion, with appropriate procedures for effective and timely input from interested parties (OECD, 1995*a*, p. 10).

Additionally, in its report on "Regulatory Quality and Public Sector Reform", the Public Management service of OECD concluded that, if regulatory reform is to be successful, regulatory reform management capacities should be strengthened and RIA should be integrated within an effective *regulatory reform management system* (see Box 13).

These features of current OECD approaches to regulatory reform and regulatory impact analysis are reflected in the proposals below which are presented for further consideration.

4.6 Recommendations

Whilst considerable advances have been made in environmental regulatory reform in OECD Member countries during the past decade, as in the case of general regulatory reform, further progress is needed.

To assist in this, two related developments would be helpful:

- strengthening the methods, procedures and practice of *regulatory impact analysis* as a tool of environmental regulation appraisal and evaluation;

- strengthening *regulatory reform management capacities* to support the timely and effective use of RIA as an integral component of the environmental regulatory reform process.

Developments in regulatory impact analysis should:

- encourage the greater use of *cost-benefit frameworks*, incorporating performance indicators relating to environmental effectiveness, cost-effectiveness, indirect economic and environmental impacts and distributional consequences;
- be useful in both *ex ante* appraisal and *ex post* evaluation;
- be applicable at *different levels* of regulatory activity (international, regional, national and local);
- be applicable to *packages* of different types of environmental regulations, as well as to individual regulations;
- increase opportunities to make better use of different types of regulatory impact information, both *quantitative* (economic *and* physical) and *qualitative*;
- encourage greater *transparency* and more effective use of *consultation* in the ERR process; and
- strengthen provisions for *quality control*, particularly *external* quality control, in the ERR process.

Additionally, developments to strengthen *regulatory reform management capacities* should assist in:

- securing the necessary level of support, *at higher levels of government and public administration*, for the regulatory reform process itself, both generally and in relation to ERR more specifically;
- ensuring that impacts which arise from *linkages between the environmental sector and other sectors*, are satisfactorily taken into account in both ERR and general RR; and
- ensuring that RIAs are not marginalised as technical exercises but are satisfactorily integrated into programming and decision-making within the ERR and RR process.

A final consideration is how a future OECD *work programme* might assist these developments. The following proposals build upon work that has already been undertaken, through collaboration between Member countries and the Environment Directorate, and use similar study methods to those previously employed.

1. There should be a continuation of the work, already undertaken in the study *Evaluating Economic Instruments for Environmental Policy* but extended in scope to cover *a*) both *ex ante appraisal* and *ex post evaluations* and *b*) *packages* containing different types of policy instruments (*e.g.* command and control, planning/voluntary agreements as well as economic instruments).

2. *Evaluation studies* could be undertaken *of* RIA *methods* already being applied to environmental regulatory systems in different Member countries and at the international level. These might include a number of country case studies, involving countries with different environmental regulatory systems and RIA experiences.

3. *Institutional case studies*, could also be undertaken, in different Member countries and at the international or regional level, concerning *a*) how RIAs are being organised, managed and used within the ERR process, *b*) how the ERR process and the general RR process are related and being co-ordinated, and *c*) how regulatory reform management capacities (both general and environmental) are being developed to improve the effectiveness of ERR and RR processes.

4. Arising from the above, the preparation of *guidance on best practices* in RIA and the management of environmental regulatory reform is also recommended.

Annex

Box A.1.   **Globalisation, institutional change
and environmental regulatory reform**

The globalisation of economic activities has been stimulated by trade and capital flow liberalisation, the growth of trans-national enterprises etc. At the same time, the significance of trans-boundary, regional and global environmental problems has grown. This has led to the increasing involvement of all Member countries in international level, environmental regulation activities. This is observable in the Environmental Performance Reviews of individual OECD Member countries, each of which contains a separate chapter dealing with these activities and, in summary form, in OECD, 1996*c*.

The institutional arrangements for regulatory activities in most Member countries are quite complex. For example,

"Government administration in the United Kingdom is carried out by over 30 national and territorial departments headed by ministers, boards or appointed officials; over 70 free-standing Executive Agencies accountable to ministries; 375 public bodies, such as single-industry regulators, not attached to ministries; 56 counties and regional councils; and about 450 district councils. Many of these bodies regulate or enforce regulations [including environmental regulations]. To this must be added the European Community, which produces a substantial amount of regulation applicable in the United Kingdom" (OECD, 1997*a*).

Changes in institutional arrangements, which affect the environmental regulatory system, may occur for non-environmental as well as environmental reasons; for example, as a response to the globalisation of economic activities mentioned above, the "contracting out" of certain regulatory activities as part of a privatisation programme, the reduced funding of central government administrative activities or other pressures to decentralise regulatory activities to more local administrative bodies.

Box A.2. **Environment Canada: regulatory review, 1992-94**

The Review covered 38 regulations relating to environmental protection and wildlife conservation.

It involved an External Advisory Panel (composed of representatives from business, labour, environmental and conservation groups and industry organisations), review teams (composed of departmental experts), a Departmental Regulatory Review office. Comments were invited from 2000 groups and individuals and public consultations took place, based upon two documents containing the findings and draft recommendations which emerged from the Review.

The principal findings of the Review were:

- the objectives of the majority of the regulations were still valid and no significant competitiveness issues arose from the Review; but

- a number of areas of overlap and duplication were identified between provincial and federal regulations;

- opportunities for streamlining, simplification and consolidation were apparent in several areas;

- five regulations could be revoked and three of these replaced by alternative instruments;

- there was some potential for using economic and voluntary instruments in combination with seven of the regulations.

An Action Plan was prepared on the basis of the Review findings. In December 1994 an overall regulatory reform programme, encompassing all government departments, was initiated under the title of *Building a More Innovative Economy*.

Source: Environment Canada (1994), *Environment Canada: Regulatory Review* (Final Report).

Box A.3. **Environmental regulatory reform in the European Union**

The European Commission has embarked on a process of reviewing the main body of EU environmental legislation with a view to:
- consolidation and streamlining
- improving ease of implementation
- removing unnecessary and costly bureaucratic procedures
- determining more cost-effective approaches
- increasing the use of market-based instruments.

● The number of new items of environmental legislation, proposed by the Commission, progressively fell from 12 in 1993, to 6 in 1995, and rose to 11 in 1996.

● Regulations are being reviewed in all major areas of environmental policy but, in the main, the aim is not to replace regulation but to modify its content and support it through the use of a broader range of instruments, notably economic instruments and voluntary agreements.

Source: EC response to Environment Directorate's Regulatory Reform Survey (1996) and supporting documentation.

Box A.4. **Some characteristics of industrial permitting systems in OECD countries**

- Both technology-based (BAT) and environmental quality-based (EQS) regulations now co-exist in most of the 18 Member countries surveyed.

- Best available technology criteria almost never mandate the use of a particular technology but are couched in terms of performance requirements. However, where the mandated performance can only be attained by a particular technology this amounts to prescribing a particular technology. Also technological criteria, when rigidly applied, ignore variations in local environmental conditions.

- The environmental quality approach is more sensitive to variations in local environmental condition. However, it may be much less easy for the authorities to determine the substances being discharged from industrial sources into the environment when using this approach rather than the BAT approach.

- The degree of discretion enjoyed by authorities in permit-setting differs between countries, being much greater in certain European countries and elsewhere than, for example, in the USA. In the former cases, the limitations of a technologically over-rigid approach to permitting may be avoided, *i.e.* variations in local environmental conditions and differing economic circumstances (see below) can be taken into account.

- In the case of the UK, the costs of BAT can properly be modified by economic considerations where the costs of applying best available techniques would be excessive in relation to the nature of the industry and the environmental protection to be achieved. The cost of the best available techniques must be weighed against the environmental damage for the process; the greater the environmental damage, the greater the costs of BAT that can be required before costs are considered excessive.

- In the case of New Zealand, economic considerations are embedded in the definition of the best practicable option upon which resource management has to be based. Economic considerations are important in determining the BPO for a specific situation but the financial capacity of a particular company to finance the works is given little consideration.

Source: OECD (1996*d*), "Environmental Requirements for Industrial Permitting: Regulatory Framework in OECD Countries – A Reference Guide" (mimeo).

Box A.5. **Integrated pollution prevention and control in OECD countries**

- The main objective of IPPC is to achieve an efficient decoupling of natural resource use, risks from hazardous substances and pollutant releases from value added by production, use and disposition of goods and services. "Efficient" means that the environmental objectives are to be obtained in the most cost-effective ways.

- A complete IPPC system includes:
  - a broadly accepted plan to reduce total resource use and energy, hazardous substances and pollutant releases;
  - means to identify broad areas for priority action;
  - use of integrated permits and a mix of other instruments to promote de-coupling in an equitable fashion;
  - acting to promote transformation to cleaner products and services in all sectors;
  - arrangements for sharing of responsibility throughout the life cycle of a given product (*e.g.* extended producer responsibility);
  - involving affected and interested parties in devising the IPC approach to be used;
  - use of appropriate indicators to measure results and provide feedback about progress.

- Several Member countries have adopted IPPC legislation, mainly relating to integrated permitting systems, which make regulatory provisions for parts of a complete IPPC system. These include Denmark, Sweden, France, Netherlands, USA, United Kingdom, Flanders (Belgium), Finland, Ireland, Italy and Japan. Additionally, Council Directive 96/61/EC, concerning integrated pollution prevention and control, was adopted by the Council of the European Union in September 1996. Member states of the EU are required to adopt the necessary legal measures to implement its provisions within three years.

Sources: i) OECD (1996e), "Integrated Pollution Prevention and Control: the Status of Member Country Implementation of Council Recommendation C(90)164/Final"; ii) "Council Directive 96/61/EC concerning integrated pollution prevention and control", *Official Journal of the European Communities* L257/26-40 (10.10.96).

REFERENCES

BARDE, J.Ph. and SMITH, St. (1997), "Do Economic Instruments Help the Environment?", *The* OECD *Observer*, No. 204, February/March 1997.

BARDE, J.Ph. (1997), "Green Taxation", *The* OECD *Observer*, Special Edition on Sustainable Development, June 1997.

COMMISSION OF THE EUROPEAN COMMUNITIES (1993), "Report from the Commission of the Implementation of Directive 85/337/EEC on the Assessment of the Effects of Certain Public and Private Projects on the Environment", COM(193)28 final, Vols. 1-13, Office for Official Publications of the European Communities, Luxembourg.

DRI (1994), "Potential Benefits of Integration of Environmental Policies: An Incentive-Based Approach to Policy Integration", Graham and Trotman/CEC, London.

EMERY, R.W. (1996), "From Extended Producer Responsibility to Shared Product Responsibility: Legal Considerations", OECD, Paris (mimeo).

ENVIRONMENT CANADA (1994), *Regulatory Review, Final Report*, Environment Canada, Ottawa.

ENVIRONMENT DIRECTORATE (1996), "Environmental Regulation: The Third Generation", ENV/EPOC/RD(96) (mimeo).

HOPKINS, T.D. (1996), "Alternative Approaches to Regulatory Analysis: Designs from Seven OECD Countries", Meeting on Regulatory Impact Analysis, May 1996, PMS/OECD, Paris.

LEE, N. (1995), "Environmental Impact Assessment Activities in OECD Countries", Report prepared for OECD Environment Directorate (mimeo).

LIPSEY, R.E. AND LANCASTER, K. (1956), "The general theory of the second best", *Review of Economic Studies*, 24, 11-32.

MINISTRY OF HOUSING, PHYSICAL PLANNING AND ENVIRONMENT (1995), "Company Environmental Management as a basis for a different relationship between companies and government authorities: a guide for Government Authorities and Companies", Draft report. MHPPE, The Hague (mimeo).

OECD (1987), *Improving the Enforcement of Environmental Policies*, Environment Monograph No. 8, OECD, Paris.

OECD (1989), *Economic Instruments for Environmental Protection*, OECD, Paris.

OECD (1991*a*), "Communiqué of the Meeting of the Environment Policy Committee at Ministerial Level", Dec. 1991, OECD, Paris.

OECD (1991*b*), *Environmental Policy: How to Apply Economic Instruments*, OECD, Paris.

OECD (1991*c*), "Recommendation of the Council on the Use of Economic Instruments in Environmental Policy", 31 January 1991, OECD, Paris.

OECD (1992*a*), *Reduction and Recycling of Packaging Waste*, Environment Monograph No. 62, OECD, Paris.

OECD (1992*b*), *Applying Economic Instruments to Packaging Waste: Practical Issues for Product Charges and Deposit-Refund Systems*, Environment Monograph No. 82, OECD, Paris.

OECD (1993), *Taxation and Environment: Complementary Policies*, OECD, Paris.

OECD (1994*a*), *Reducing Environmental Pollution: Looking Back, Thinking Ahead*, OECD, Paris.

OECD (1994*b*), *Managing the Environment: the Role of Economic Instruments*, OECD, Paris.

OECD (1994*c*), *The Economics of Climate Change*, OECD, Paris.

OECD (1994*d*), *The Environmental Effects of Trade*, OECD, Paris.

OECD (1995*a*), "Recommendation of the Council of the OECD on Improving the Quality of Government Regulation", (Adopted on 9 March 1995), OECD/GD(95)95, OECD, Paris.

OECD (1995*b*), *Environmental Taxes in OECD Countries*, OECD, Paris.

OECD (1995*c*), *The Life Cycle Approach: An Overview of Product/Process Analysis*, OECD, Paris.

OECD (1996*a*), *Regulatory Reform: Overview and Proposed OECD Work Plan*, OECD/GD(96)115, OECD, Paris.

OECD (1996*b*), "Meeting of the Council at Ministerial Level, May 1996: Communiqué", OECD, Paris.

OECD (1996*c*), *Environmental Performance in OECD Countries: Progress in the 1990s*, OECD, Paris.

OECD (1996*d*), *Environmental Requirements for Industrial Permitting: Regulatory Framework in OECD Countries – A Reference Guide*, Draft Report, OECD, Paris (mimeo).

OECD (1996*e*), "Integrated Pollution Prevention and Control: the Status of Member Country Implementation of Council Recommendation", C(90)164/Final, OECD, Paris.

OECD (1996*f*), *Implementation Strategies for Environmental Taxes*, OECD, Paris.

OECD (1996*g*), *Saving Biological Diversity: Economic Incentives*, OECD, Paris.

OECD (1996h), *Extended Producer Responsibility in the OECD Area: Phase I Report*, OECD, Paris.

OECD (1996i), "Case Study: Responsible Care Initiative", Labour Management Programme Meeting, November 1996, PMS/OECD, Paris (mimeo).

OECD (1996j), "The Economy-Wide Effects of Regulatory Reform", Economics Department, OECD, Paris (mimeo).

OECD (1996k), "Regulatory Reform, Industrial Competitiveness and Innovation", Directorate for Science, Technology and Industry, OECD, Paris (mimeo).

OECD (1996l), "Competition Policy and Environment", Committee on Competition Law and Policy, OECD, Paris.

OECD (1996m), "Regulatory Reform and the Agro-Food Sector", Draft Report, Directorate for Food, Agriculture and Fisheries, OECD, Paris.

OECD (1996n), "Product Standards, Conformity Assessment and Regulatory Reform", Draft Report, Trade Directorate, OECD, Paris.

OECD (1996o), *Integrating Environment and Economy: Progress in the 1990s*, OECD, Paris.

OECD (1996p), *Overview of Regulatory Impact Analysis in OECD Countries: Note by Public Management Service Secretariat for Meeting on Regulatory Impact Analysis*, May 1996, OECD, Paris.

OECD (1996q), *Environmental Performance Review: United States*, OECD, Paris.

OECD/IEA (1996), "Voluntary Actions for Energy-Related CO_2 Abatement", Draft Report, OECD/IEA, Paris (mimeo).

OECD (1997a), *Regulatory Quality and Public Sector Reform*, OECD, Paris.

OECD (1997b), *Evaluating Economic Instruments for Environmental Policy*, OECD, Paris.

OECD (1997c), *Environmental Policies and Employment*, OECD, Paris.

OECD (1997d), *Environmental Taxes and Green Tax Reform*, OECD, Paris.

OECD (1997e), *Regulatory Reform in the Electricity Sector*, OECD, Paris.

OECD (1997f), *Regulatory Impact Analysis: Best Practices in OECD Countries*, OECD, Paris.

PALMER, K., OATES, W. E. and PORTNEY, P.R. (1995), "Tightening Environmental Standards: The Benefit-Cost or the No-Cost Paradigm?", *Journal of Economic Perspectives*, 9, 4, 119-32.

PORTER, M.E. and VAN DER LINDEN, C. (1995), "Toward a New Conception of the Environment – Competitiveness Relationship", *Journal of Economic Perspectives*, 9, 4, 97-118.

REPETTO, R. *et al.* (1996), *Has Environmental Protection Really Reduced Productivity Growth?* World Resources Institute, Washington, DC., USA.

STOREY, M. (1996), "Demand Side Efficiency: Voluntary Agreements with Industry", Policies and Measures for Common Action, Working Paper No. 8, OECD/IEA, Paris (mimeo).

TIETENBERG, T.H. (1990), "Economic Instruments for Environmental Regulation", *Oxford Review of Economic Policy*, 6,1, p. 24.

USEPA (1996), *Re-inventing Environmental Regulation*, US Environmental Protection Agency Washington DC, USA.

MAIN SALES OUTLETS OF OECD PUBLICATIONS
PRINCIPAUX POINTS DE VENTE DES PUBLICATIONS DE L'OCDE

AUSTRALIA – AUSTRALIE
D.A. Information Services
648 Whitehorse Road, P.O.B 163
Mitcham, Victoria 3132   Tel. (03) 9210.7777
                         Fax: (03) 9210.7788

AUSTRIA – AUTRICHE
Gerold & Co.
Graben 31
Wien I   Tel. (0222) 533.50.14
                    Fax: (0222) 512.47.31.29

BELGIUM – BELGIQUE
Jean De Lannoy
Avenue du Roi, Koningslaan 202
B-1060 Bruxelles Tel. (02) 538.51.69/538.08.41
                         Fax: (02) 538.08.41

CANADA
Renouf Publishing Company Ltd.
5369 Canotek Road
Unit 1
Ottawa, Ont. K1J 9J3   Tel. (613) 745.2665
                         Fax: (613) 745.7660

Stores:
71 1/2 Sparks Street
Ottawa, Ont. K1P 5R1   Tel. (613) 238.8985
                         Fax: (613) 238.6041

12 Adelaide Street West
Toronto, QN M5H 1L6   Tel. (416) 363.3171
                       Fax: (416) 363.5963

Les Éditions La Liberté Inc.
3020 Chemin Sainte-Foy
Sainte-Foy, PQ G1X 3V6 Tel. (418) 658.3763
                       Fax: (418) 658.3763

Federal Publications Inc.
165 University Avenue, Suite 701
Toronto, ON M5H 3B8   Tel. (416) 860.1611
                      Fax: (416) 860.1608

Les Publications Fédérales
1185 Université
Montréal, QC H3B 3A7   Tel. (514) 954.1633
                       Fax: (514) 954.1635

CHINA – CHINE
Book Dept., China Natinal Publications
Import and Export Corporation (CNPIEC)
16 Gongti E. Road, Chaoyang District
Beijing 100020 Tel. (10) 6506-6688 Ext. 8402
                          (10) 6506-3101

CHINESE TAIPEI – TAIPEI CHINOIS
Good Faith Worldwide Int'l. Co. Ltd.
9th Floor, No. 118, Sec. 2
Chung Hsiao E. Road
Taipei   Tel. (02) 391.7396/391.7397
                    Fax: (02) 394.9176

**CZECH REPUBLIC –
RÉPUBLIQUE TCHÈQUE**
National Information Centre
NIS – prodejna
Konviktská 5
Praha 1 – 113 57   Tel. (02) 24.23.09.07
                   Fax: (02) 24.22.94.33
E-mail: nkposp@dec.niz.cz
Internet: http://www.nis.cz

DENMARK – DANEMARK
Munksgaard Book and Subscription Service
35, Nørre Søgade, P.O. Box 2148
DK-1016 København K   Tel. (33) 12.85.70
                        Fax: (33) 12.93.87

J. H. Schultz Information A/S,
Herstedvang 12,
DK – 2620 Albertslung   Tel. 43 63 23 00
                         Fax: 43 63 19 69
Internet: s-info@inet.uni-c.dk

EGYPT – ÉGYPTE
The Middle East Observer
41 Sherif Street
Cairo   Tel. (2) 392.6919
                    Fax: (2) 360.6804

FINLAND – FINLANDE
Akateeminen Kirjakauppa
Keskuskatu 1, P.O. Box 128
00100 Helsinki

Subscription Services/Agence d'abonnements :
P.O. Box 23
00100 Helsinki   Tel. (358) 9.121.4403
                        Fax: (358) 9.121.4450

***FRANCE**
OECD/OCDE
Mail Orders/Commandes par correspondance :
2, rue André-Pascal
75775 Paris Cedex 16 Tel. 33 (0)1.45.24.82.00
                     Fax: 33 (0)1.49.10.42.76
                     Telex: 640048 OCDE
Internet: Compte.PUBSINQ@oecd.org

Orders via Minitel, France only/
Commandes par Minitel, France
exclusivement : 36 15 OCDE

OECD Bookshop/Librairie de l'OCDE :
33, rue Octave-Feuillet
75016 Paris   Tel. 33 (0)1.45.24.81.81
                          33 (0)1.45.24.81.67

Dawson
B.P. 40
91121 Palaiseau Cedex   Tel. 01.89.10.47.00
                        Fax: 01.64.54.83.26

Documentation Française
29, quai Voltaire
75007 Paris   Tel. 01.40.15.70.00

Economica
49, rue Héricart
75015 Paris   Tel. 01.45.78.12.92
                        Fax: 01.45.75.05.67

Gibert Jeune (Droit-Économie)
6, place Saint-Michel
75006 Paris   Tel. 01.43.25.91.19

Librairie du Commerce International
10, avenue d'Iéna
75016 Paris   Tel. 01.40.73.34.60

Librairie Dunod
Université Paris-Dauphine
Place du Maréchal-de-Lattre-de-Tassigny
75016 Paris   Tel. 01.44.05.40.13

Librairie Lavoisier
11, rue Lavoisier
75008 Paris   Tel. 01.42.65.39.95

Librairie des Sciences Politiques
30, rue Saint-Guillaume
75007 Paris   Tel. 01.45.48.36.02

P.U.F.
49, boulevard Saint-Michel
75005 Paris   Tel. 01.43.25.83.40

Librairie de l'Université
12a, rue Nazareth
13100 Aix-en-Provence   Tel. 04.42.26.18.08

Documentation Française
165, rue Garibaldi
69003 Lyon   Tel. 04.78.63.32.23

Librairie Decitre
29, place Bellecour
69002 Lyon   Tel. 04.72.40.54.54

Librairie Sauramps
Le Triangle
34967 Montpellier Cedex 2 Tel. 04.67.58.85.15
                        Fax: 04.67.58.27.36

A la Sorbonne Actual
23, rue de l'Hôtel-des-Postes
06000 Nice   Tel. 04.93.13.77.75
                      Fax: 04.93.80.75.69

GERMANY – ALLEMAGNE
OECD Bonn Centre
August-Bebel-Allee 6
D-53175 Bonn   Tel. (0228) 959.120
                        Fax: (0228) 959.12.17

GREECE – GRÈCE
Librairie Kauffmann
Stadiou 28
10564 Athens   Tel. (01) 32.55.321
                        Fax: (01) 32.30.320

HONG-KONG
Swindon Book Co. Ltd.
Astoria Bldg. 3F
34 Ashley Road, Tsimshatsui
Kowloon, Hong Kong   Tel. 2376.2062
                        Fax: 2376.0685

HUNGARY – HONGRIE
Euro Info Service
Margitsziget, Európa Ház
1138 Budapest   Tel. (1) 111.60.61
                        Fax: (1) 302.50.35
E-mail: euroinfo@mail.matav.hu
Internet: http://www.euroinfo.hu//index.html

ICELAND – ISLANDE
Mál og Menning
Laugavegi 18, Pósthólf 392
121 Reykjavik   Tel. (1) 552.4240
                        Fax: (1) 562.3523

INDIA – INDE
Oxford Book and Stationery Co.
Scindia House
New Delhi 110001   Tel. (11) 331.5896/5308
                    Fax: (11) 332.2639
E-mail: oxford.publ@axcess.net.in

17 Park Street
Calcutta 700016   Tel. 240832

INDONESIA – INDONÉSIE
Pdii-Lipi
P.O. Box 4298
Jakarta 12042   Tel. (21) 573.34.67
                        Fax: (21) 573.34.67

IRELAND – IRLANDE
Government Supplies Agency
Publications Section
4/5 Harcourt Road
Dublin 2   Tel. 661.31.11
                        Fax: 475.27.60

ISRAEL – ISRAËL
Praedicta
5 Shatner Street
P.O. Box 34030
Jerusalem 91430   Tel. (2) 652.84.90/1/2
                        Fax: (2) 652.84.93

R.O.Y. International
P.O. Box 13056
Tel Aviv 61130   Tel. (3) 546 1423
                        Fax: (3) 546 1442
E-mail: royil@netvision.net.il

Palestinian Authority/Middle East:
INDEX Information Services
P.O.B. 19502
Jerusalem   Tel. (2) 627.16.34
                        Fax: (2) 627.12.19

ITALY – ITALIE
Libreria Commissionaria Sansoni
Via Duca di Calabria, 1/1
50125 Firenze   Tel. (055) 64.54.15
                        Fax: (055) 64.12.57
E-mail: licosa@ftbcc.it

Via Bartolini 29
20155 Milano   Tel. (02) 36.50.83

Editrice e Libreria Herder
Piazza Montecitorio 120
00186 Roma   Tel. 679.46.28
                        Fax: 678.47.51

Libreria Hoepli
Via Hoepli 5
20121 Milano Tel. (02) 86.54.46
Fax: (02) 805.28.86
Libreria Scientifica
Dott. Lucio de Biasio 'Aeiou'
Via Coronelli, 6
20146 Milano Tel. (02) 48.95.45.52
Fax: (02) 48.95.45.48

JAPAN – JAPON
OECD Tokyo Centre
Landic Akasaka Building
2-3-4 Akasaka, Minato-ku
Tokyo 107 Tel. (81.3) 3586.2016
Fax: (81.3) 3584.7929

KOREA – CORÉE
Kyobo Book Centre Co. Ltd.
P.O. Box 1658, Kwang Hwa Moon
Seoul Tel. 730.78.91
Fax: 735.00.30

MALAYSIA – MALAISIE
University of Malaya Bookshop
University of Malaya
P.O. Box 1127, Jalan Pantai Baru
59700 Kuala Lumpur
Malaysia Tel. 756.5000/756.5425
Fax: 756.3246

MEXICO – MEXIQUE
OECD Mexico Centre
Edificio INFOTEC
Av. San Fernando no. 37
Col. Toriello Guerra
Tlalpan C.P. 14050
Mexico D.F. Tel. (525) 528.10.38
Fax: (525) 606.13.07
E-mail: ocde@rtn.net.mx

NETHERLANDS – PAYS-BAS
SDU Uitgeverij Plantijnstraat
Externe Fondsen
Postbus 20014
2500 EA's-Gravenhage Tel. (070) 37.89.880
Voor bestellingen: Fax: (070) 34.75.778

Subscription Agency/Agence d'abonnements :
SWETS & ZEITLINGER BV
Heereweg 347B
P.O. Box 830
2160 SZ Lisse Tel. 252.435.111
Fax: 252.415.888

**NEW ZEALAND –
NOUVELLE-ZÉLANDE**
GPLegislation Services
P.O. Box 12418
Thorndon, Wellington Tel. (04) 496.5655
Fax: (04) 496.5698

NORWAY – NORVÈGE
NIC INFO A/S
Ostensjoveien 18
P.O. Box 6512 Etterstad
0606 Oslo Tel. (22) 97.45.00
Fax: (22) 97.45.45

PAKISTAN
Mirza Book Agency
65 Shahrah Quaid-E-Azam
Lahore 54000 Tel. (42) 735.36.01
Fax: (42) 576.37.14

PHILIPPINE – PHILIPPINES
International Booksource Center Inc.
Rm 179/920 Cityland 10 Condo Tower 2
HV dela Costa Ext cor Valero St.
Makati Metro Manila Tel. (632) 817 9676
Fax: (632) 817 1741

POLAND – POLOGNE
Ars Polona
00-950 Warszawa
Krakowskie Prezdmiescie 7 Tel. (22) 264760
Fax: (22) 265334

PORTUGAL
Livraria Portugal
Rua do Carmo 70-74
Apart. 2681
1200 Lisboa Tel. (01) 347.49.82/5
Fax: (01) 347.02.64

SINGAPORE – SINGAPOUR
Ashgate Publishing
Asia Pacific Pte. Ltd
Golden Wheel Building, 04-03
41, Kallang Pudding Road
Singapore 349316 Tel. 741.5166
Fax: 742.9356

SPAIN – ESPAGNE
Mundi-Prensa Libros S.A.
Castelló 37, Apartado 1223
Madrid 28001 Tel. (91) 431.33.99
Fax: (91) 575.39.98
E-mail: mundiprensa@tsai.es
Internet: http://www.mundiprensa.es

Mundi-Prensa Barcelona
Consell de Cent No. 391
08009 – Barcelona Tel. (93) 488.34.92
Fax: (93) 487.76.59

Libreria de la Generalitat
Palau Moja
Rambla dels Estudis, 118
08002 – Barcelona
(Suscripciones) Tel. (93) 318.80.12
(Publicaciones) Tel. (93) 302.67.23
Fax: (93) 412.18.54

SRI LANKA
Centre for Policy Research
c/o Colombo Agencies Ltd.
No. 300-304, Galle Road
Colombo 3 Tel. (1) 574240, 573551-2
Fax: (1) 575394, 510711

SWEDEN – SUÈDE
CE Fritzes AB
S–106 47 Stockholm Tel. (08) 690.90.90
Fax: (08) 20.50.21

For electronic publications only/
Publications électroniques seulement
STATISTICS SWEDEN
Informationsservice
S-115 81 Stockholm Tel. 8 783 5066
Fax: 8 783 4045

Subscription Agency/Agence d'abonnements :
Wennergren-Williams Info AB
P.O. Box 1305
171 25 Solna Tel. (08) 705.97.50
Fax: (08) 27.00.71

Liber distribution
Internatinal organizations
Fagerstagatan 21
S-163 52 Spanga

SWITZERLAND – SUISSE
Maditec S.A. (Books and Periodicals/Livres
et périodiques)
Chemin des Palettes 4
Case postale 266
1020 Renens VD 1 Tel. (021) 635.08.65
Fax: (021) 635.07.80

Librairie Payot S.A.
4, place Pépinet
CP 3212
1002 Lausanne Tel. (021) 320.25.11
Fax: (021) 320.25.14

Librairie Unilivres
6, rue de Candolle
1205 Genève Tel. (022) 320.26.23
Fax: (022) 329.73.18

Subscription Agency/Agence d'abonnements :
Dynapresse Marketing S.A.
38, avenue Vibert
1227 Carouge Tel. (022) 308.08.70
Fax: (022) 308.07.99
See also – Voir aussi :
OECD Bonn Centre
August-Bebel-Allee 6
D-53175 Bonn (Germany) Tel. (0228) 959.120
Fax: (0228) 959.12.17

THAILAND – THAÏLANDE
Suksit Siam Co. Ltd.
113, 115 Fuang Nakhon Rd.
Opp. Wat Rajbopith
Bangkok 10200 Tel. (662) 225.9531/2
Fax: (662) 222.5188

**TRINIDAD & TOBAGO, CARIBBEAN
TRINITÉ-ET-TOBAGO, CARAÏBES**
Systematics Studies Limited
9 Watts Street
Curepe
Trinidad & Tobago, W.I. Tel. (1809) 645.3475
Fax: (1809) 662.5654
E-mail: tobe@trinidad.net

TUNISIA – TUNISIE
Grande Librairie Spécialisée
Fendri Ali
Avenue Haffouz Imm El-Intilaka
Bloc B 1 Sfax 3000 Tel. (216-4) 296 855
Fax: (216-4) 298.270

TURKEY – TURQUIE
Kültür Yayinlari Is-Türk Ltd.
Atatürk Bulvari No. 191/Kat 13
06684 Kavaklidere/Ankara
Tel. (312) 428.11.40 Ext. 2458
Fax : (312) 417.24.90
Dolmabahce Cad. No. 29
Besiktas/Istanbul Tel. (212) 260 7188

UNITED KINGDOM – ROYAUME-UNI
The Stationery Office Ltd.
Postal orders only:
P.O. Box 276, London SW8 5DT
Gen. enquiries Tel. (171) 873 0011
Fax: (171) 873 8463
The Stationery Office Ltd.
Postal orders only:
49 High Holborn, London WC1V 6HB
Branches at: Belfast, Birmingham, Bristol,
Edinburgh, Manchester

UNITED STATES – ÉTATS-UNIS
OECD Washington Center
2001 L Street N.W., Suite 650
Washington, D.C. 20036-4922
Tel. (202) 785.6323
Fax: (202) 785.0350
Internet: washcont@oecd.org

Subscriptions to OECD periodicals may also
be placed through main subscription agencies.

Les abonnements aux publications périodiques
de l'OCDE peuvent être souscrits auprès des
principales agences d'abonnement.

Orders and inquiries from countries where Distributors have not yet been appointed should be
sent to: OECD Publications, 2, rue André-Pascal, 75775 Paris Cedex 16, France.

Les commandes provenant de pays où l'OCDE
n'a pas encore désigné de distributeur peuvent
être adressées aux Éditions de l'OCDE, 2, rue
André-Pascal, 75775 Paris Cedex 16, France.

12-1996

OECD PUBLICATIONS, 2, rue André-Pascal, 75775 PARIS CEDEX 16
PRINTED IN FRANCE
(97 97 07 1 P) ISBN 92-64-15513-9 – No. 49515 1997